"With crisp, engaging prose, Morris, Mayer, Kenter, and Anderson explore the ways in which policymaking in the southern states remains distinct and the ways in which it has converged with the rest of the nation. This volume is essential reading for anyone who wants to understand policymaking in our federal system or the enduring legacy of the American South."

Christopher Cooper, *Madison Distinguished Professor, Western Carolina University*

"Over the past seven decades, scholars of southern politics have tended to focus their intellectual curiosity and studies on elections in the South. Since that time, Morris, Mayer, Kenter, and Anderson have taken an innovative new approach in which they seek to answer the question of whether policy differences exist between southern and non-southern states. This work takes the study of southern politics away solely from elections and helps to shed light on the regional impacts in the formation of public policy."

Scott E. Buchanan, *Professor of Political Science, Georgia College & State University*

"John Morris and colleagues have provided an excellent addition to the literature on southern politics, especially in the underdeveloped area of policy making in the South. The book offers an insightful analysis of southern distinctiveness along with how we define the South. The authors provide a compelling model of state policy making by utilizing a common set of explanatory factors (political variables, socioeconomic conditions, and state need) to explore policy development in six very timely and highly relevant policy arenas ranging from the Affordable Care Act to reproductive rights of women to state firearm legislation to fatal police violence to the pandemic response. *Policy Making and Southern Distinctiveness* is an excellent addition to not only classes on southern politics but also courses on federalism as well as policy development and policy analysis."

James T. LaPlant, *Professor of Political Science, Dean of the College of Humanities and Social Sciences, Valdosta State University*

"A great deal of ink has been spilt analyzing southern distinctiveness. We know that the South is different ideologically, racially, culturally, and more monolithic in its voting preferences than the rest of nation. The authors seek to discover if the uniqueness of the South has real policy implications. Their research confirms that despite the ongoing homogenization of the United States, the South retains a unique approach in addressing many pressing public issues. *Policy Making and Southern Distinctiveness* is a timely and valuable contribution to the study of southern politics and the role of region in state level policymaking."

DuBose Kapeluck, *Co-Director, The Citadel Symposium on Southern Politics*

"In *Policy Making and Southern Distinctiveness*, Morris, Mayer, Kenter, and Anderson provide a sorely needed examination of whether the contemporary American South remains differentiable in the laws it passes. Through detailed analyses of several of the most salient issues in American politics (e.g., regulation of firearms, abortion, and the Affordable Care Act) from 2012 to 2018, the southern states take actions that reflect the persistence of its more conservative political culture. This is a must-read for scholars interested in the connection between politics and policymaking."

Seth C. McKee, *Oklahoma State University*

Policy Making and Southern Distinctiveness

Policy Making and Southern Distinctiveness examines the uniqueness of southern politics and their policy choices.

While decades of scholarship on the politics of the American South have focused on partisanship and electoral outcomes as the primary elements of interest in southern politics, few works have focused on the more practical outcomes of these political processes, specifically, comparing state policy choices of southern states to non-southern states. This book examines six different policy arenas: voting access, gun control, health care, reproductive rights, water, and COVID-19 pandemic response, comparing policy choices in states in the South with states in the non-South. The authors find that the South is distinct in several, but not all, of the policy arenas examined. They conclude that the South as a region is unique because of the exceptional degree of one-party control evident in the South, coupled with a long-standing preoccupation with partisanship and race-based politics.

Policy Making and Southern Distinctiveness provides valuable insights into how and why states behave in the manner they do and where southern states may diverge from the rest of the country. It will be of interest to scholars of southern politics, state comparative policy, public policy, American politics, and federalism/intergovernmental relations.

John C. Morris is a professor in the Department of Political Science at Auburn University. He previously served as a faculty member at Mississippi State University and Old Dominion University. He has studied southern politics and policy for more than 25 years and has published widely in the fields of political science, public administration, and public policy. He is the coeditor of *Speaking Green with a Southern Accent: Environmental Management and Innovation in the South* (2010) and *True Green: Executive Effectiveness in the US Environmental Protection Agency* (2012). He is coeditor of *Building the Local Economy: Cases in Economic Development* (2008); coeditor of a three-volume series *Prison Privatization: The Many*

Facets of a Controversial Industry (2012); and *Advancing Collaboration Theory: Models, Typologies, and Evidence* (Routledge, 2016). His most recent books include *The Case for Grassroots Collaboration: Social Capital and Ecosystem Restoration at the Local Level* (2013, with others); *State Politics and the Affordable Care Act: Choices and Decisions* (Routledge, 2019, with others); *Organizational Motivation for Collaboration: Theory and Evidence* (2019, with Luisa Diaz-Kope); *Multiorganizational Arrangements for Watershed Protection: Working Better Together* (Routledge, 2021, with Madeleine W. McNamara); and *Clean Water Policy and State Choice: Promise and Performance in the Water Quality Act* (Cambridge, forthcoming 2022). In addition, he has published more than 110 peer-reviewed articles, book chapters, and reports.

Martin K. Mayer is an assistant professor at the University of North Carolina at Pembroke (UNCP) in the Department of Political Science and Public Administration. In this position he teaches a variety of courses, primarily in the graduate school, in public management and health policy, and he leads the health administration concentration. He holds a PhD in public administration from Old Dominion University in Norfolk, Virginia, and additional degrees from the University of Akron. His previous work is centered primarily on decision-making and resource scarcity in the domains of health policy, local government, and transportation finance. He is the coauthor (with John C. Morris, Robert C. Kenter, and Luisa M. Lucero) of *State Politics and the Affordable Care Act: Choices and Decisions* (2019). His journal publications appear in *Social Science Quarterly*, *Politics & Policy*, *The Social Science Journal*, *Public Works Management and Policy*, *State and Local Government Review* and *Politics and the Life Sciences*, among others. He has contributed to several other book projects, reports, and committees on a variety of topics from sea-level rise to southern politics, public health, and environment policy.

Robert C. Kenter is the Director of Law Enforcement Field Engagement at the Center for Policing Equity, a non-profit action and research think tank. Prior to joining the Center for Policing Equity he served over 30 years with the Norfolk Police Department before retiring in April 2020. He holds a PhD in public administration from the School of Public Service at Old Dominion University, Norfolk, Virginia. His research focuses on procedural justice, southern politics, and healthcare reform. His work has appeared in *Social Science Quarterly*, *Policing: An International Journal*, and *Politics and Policy*. He is also coauthor of *State Politics and the Affordable Care Act: Choices and Decisions* (Routledge, 2019).

R. Bruce Anderson is the Dr. Sarah D. and L. Kirk McKay, Jr. Endowed Chair in American History, Government, and Civics and Miller Distinguished Professor of Political Science at Florida Southern College in Lakeland, Florida, where he teaches the American core curriculum and is director of the Pre-Law program, and has developed multiple programs in civic education for both higher education and K-12 curriculum, including developing, authoring and editing the text "Exploring the Constitution," a nonpartisan/nonideological classroom text on constitutional mechanics. He holds a PhD in political science from Rice University. He is also a columnist for the Lakeland Ledger/USA Today Network and Political Consultant and on-air commentator for WLKF Radio of Hall Communications. He is a contributor, for the last three editions, to *The New Politics of the Old South* (edited by Charles Bullock III and Mark J. Rozell) and has published essays on many disparate subjects, including state legislative politics, the political life of Strom Thurmond and the Dixiecrats, the concept of justice in Immanuel Kant (with Sarah Massey), and KGB/GRU and CIA surveillance tradecraft and techniques. His work has also appeared in *The American Review of Politics*, *The American Politics Quarterly*, *Social Science Quarterly*, as well as more "mainstream" print media outlets.

Routledge Research in Public Administration and Public Policy

The Transformative Potential of Participatory Budgeting
Creating an Ideal Democracy
George Robert Bateman Jr.

City Sextons
Tales from Municipal Leaders
Staci M. Zavattaro

Multiorganizational Arrangements for Watershed Protection
Working Better Together
John Charles Morris and Madeleine Wright McNamara

Affirmative Action in Malaysia and South Africa
Preference for Parity
Hwok-Aun Lee

Critical Perspectives on Public Systems Management in India
Through the Lens of District Administration
Amar K J R Nayak and Ram Kumar Kakani

Policy Making and Southern Distinctiveness
John C. Morris, Martin K. Mayer, Robert C. Kenter and R. Bruce Anderson

For more information about this series, please visit: www.routledge.com/Routledge-Research-in-Public-Administration-and-Public-Policy/book-series/RRPAPP

Policy Making and Southern Distinctiveness

John C. Morris, Martin K. Mayer, Robert C. Kenter and R. Bruce Anderson

R Routledge

Taylor & Francis Group

NEW YORK AND LONDON

First published 2022
by Routledge
605 Third Avenue, New York, NY 10158

and by Routledge
2 Park Square, Milton Park, Abingdon, Oxon, OX14 4RN

Routledge is an imprint of the Taylor & Francis Group, an informa business

© 2022 John C. Morris, Martin K. Mayer, Robert C. Kenter and R. Bruce Anderson

Library of Congress Cataloging-in-Publication Data
A catalog record for this title has been requested

ISBN: 978-0-367-67733-6 (hbk)
ISBN: 978-0-367-68194-4 (pbk)
ISBN: 978-1-003-13460-2 (ebk)

DOI: 10.4324/9781003134602

Typeset in Times New Roman
by Deanta Global Publishing Services, Chennai, India

This volume is dedicated to the generations of scholars who have gathered in Charleston since 1978 to further the scholarship on southern politics.

Contents

Tables

Acknowledgments

In 1978, three faculty members at the Military College of South Carolina, The Citadel, in Charleston, South Carolina, hosted a small group of scholars with an interest in southern politics. The three scholars, Tod Baker, Larry Moreland, and Robert Steed, envisioned a forum in which participants could not only share their work but that would work collectively to advance the state of knowledge in southern politics. The group agreed to meet biennially in Charleston to share their research and ideas. More than four decades later, the Citadel Symposium on Southern Politics continues to draw the most well-known scholars of southern politics across the nation. The research presented at the symposium has spawned scores of scholarly articles and more than a dozen books on southern politics.

Over the years both the participants and the organizers have changed, but the initial vision of Tod, Larry, and Bob has not. The symposium continues to be one of the best-kept secrets in political science: a conference in which the level of scholarship is exceptionally high, but one in which the participants are both engaged and supportive. This volume has its roots in the symposium – several of the chapters are developed from work presented at the symposium – and the authors of this book represent two generations of scholars of the symposium. We thank Tod, Larry, and Bob and, more recently, Scott Buchanan and DuBose Kapeluck, for their efforts to keep the symposium both alive and vibrant. This volume is very much a product of the symposium, and we are indebted to both the organizers and the participants for their contributions to this book, large and small.

We also wish to thank Zach Bauman for his intellectual contributions to the material in Chapter 2; his ideas and work are reflected in that chapter. We also thank Sarah Shannon-Mohamed for her assistance with the creation of the index for this volume. We are indebted to our editor at Routledge, Natalja Mortensen; her efforts made this a drama-free process, and we very much appreciate her support. Finally, we are indebted to our respective families for their love and support.

1 Why Study Southern Policy Making?

More than 70 years ago, V.O. Key (1949) published a book titled *Southern Politics in State and Nation*. The culmination of several years' worth of meticulous research, his goal was to better understand the politics of the South and how those political traditions emanated from the culture and history of the region. The research covered the states of the former Confederacy in great detail, even developing regional distinctions within states. Key argued the eleven former Confederate states all have individual personalities, but they act politically as one unit. He compared southern states to siblings: brothers and sisters who may have distinct dispositions but share common family traits. These shared traits include a plantation tradition that had been supported by slavery, implicit political conflicts that have been repressed by a one-party system, and the unique American experience of wartime defeat and devastation (Bass & DeVries, 1995). Key intuitively understood a fundamental dichotomy of the South as a region: although the South seemed to be cohesive as a region (and very different from the rest of the nation), he also understood that the individual southern states, and even areas within states, were unique. How could the South seemingly show such solidarity, and yet reveal so much fragmentation within the region? Was the cohesiveness strong enough to overcome the fragmentation within the South?

Key's focus was clearly on the politics of the South. At the time of Key's writing, politics in the South were dominated by a single party (the Democratic Party), and the issues of race and civil rights dominated both political and public life. Jim Crow regulations were fully in force, segregation was the law, and social, racial, and economic divisions ran deep. Key's important insight was that the South was different from the rest of the nation, in that the politics of how southern states addressed these issues was fundamentally different than that of non-South states. Single-party control, coupled with a strong conservative ideology, a cultural distrust of people outside the region, and long-standing traditions of agrarianism (Reed, 1983), racism (Acharya, Blackwell, & Sen, 2018; Black & Black, 1987),

DOI: 10.4324/9781003134602-1

religion (Baker et al., 1983; Elazar, 1972), and a healthy distrust of government combined to give the South a very distinct "personality." Moreover, this distinction mattered in ways that could be detected empirically.

Today the South is again dominated by a single party, but it is now the Republican Party. Although the labels have changed, the underlying conservative political ideology has changed little. Indeed, the 1990s saw a significant number of southern politicians switch parties without making substantial changes in their ideologies, their offices, or their constituencies. The net result was that party labels changed, but little else about the politics of the South changed. Many of the other factors considered by Key (and legions of scholars of southern politics since) are still in place, but much has changed in the South as well. Southern culture (see Cooper & Knotts, 2017) has changed as a result of years of in-migration; technological changes such as the widespread availability of television in the 1950s and 1960s, and of broadband internet service in the 1990s and 2000s have all served to alter and dilute traditional southern culture. However, in spite of these changes (or, perhaps, *because* of these changes), southern identity remains strong, and the politics of the South maintains enough distinctiveness to be of interest to scholars.

In the 70 years since the initial publication of Key's work, there has been a steady stream of scholarly work to better understand the South as a distinct political region. Key's work effectively founded the field of southern politics; one can now find courses at universities across the nation that focus on southern politics. There are textbooks specifically designed for such courses (see, e.g., McKee, 2019; Woodward, 2013). The Military College of South Carolina (The Citadel) in Charleston, South Carolina, has hosted the biennial Citadel Symposium on Southern Politics since 1978, attended regularly by the most active scholars of southern politics in the discipline. This work has found its way into mainstream journals and some of the most respected scholarly presses in the world and stands today as the single largest body of regional politics scholarship in the United States. In sum, southern politics remains a vibrant field of study, and one which strives to continue the work begun by Key more than 7 decades ago.

One of the underlying questions of this work is the degree to which the South remains politically distinct (Steed et al., 1990). This is a question of no small importance; if the South is not distinct politically from the rest of the nation, then the justification for studying the South is obviated. A region that is not distinct from other regions is thus, in essence, a distinction without a difference. On the other hand, if elements of southern distinctiveness can be detected, then the nature (and causes) of that distinctiveness become both relevant and interesting. If the South is distinct as a region, in what ways is it distinct? How does the region compare to the rest of the United

States? More importantly, do the distinctions matter in any relevant manner? If the region is distinct, but the distinctions have no practical or social-scientific basis, should we even be asking the question?

In terms of distinctiveness, the general consensus among scholars of southern politics is that yes; the South is distinct. We see patterns in election outcomes (Maxwell & Shields, 2019), redistricting (Aldrich & Griffin, 2017; Bullock, 2010), citizen ideology (Levendusky, 2009; Lublin, 2004), cultural identity (Cooper & Knotts, 2017; Wilson & Ferris, 1989), electoral preferences (Aistrup, 2010; Bass & DeVries, 1995), and partisanship (Black & Black, 1987; Campbell, 1977; Nadeu & Stanley, 1993) that show evidence that southern states are different. In addition, a less-traveled path has examined policy choices in southern states. The logic of this work is as follows: if southern states are indeed unique in terms of election outcomes, ideology, partisanship, etc., then we should be able to see those differences translate into different state policy choices. In other words, the kinds of policy preferences (and policy outcomes) sought by southern states should also be different. If policy outcomes are indeed the net result of a political process, the differences in the processes only matter if the policy outcomes are different. It is the goal of this book to examine the degree to which policy choices in the South differ from those in the rest of the nation – in essence, the degree to which politics in the South really matters at the state level.

Related to this, much of the extant work in southern politics is focused on electoral outcomes with national implications. The bulk of scholarship in this realm addresses issues such as the effects of redistricting (see Bullock, 2010), the outcomes of congressional elections (McKee, 2010), or presidential elections (Black & Black, 1992; Kapeluck et al., 2009). A smaller body of work has examined the composition of state legislatures or state gubernatorial control.[1] We do know there is a link between national-level and state-level electoral outcomes, but if the focus of the work is placed on national political outcomes, we are left with gaps in our knowledge about state politics and their effects. The lack of focus on state-level politics leaves unanswered questions about the real-world effects of those politics in the form of policy.

Luckily for scholars and students of southern politics, it does appear that the South retains at least some uniqueness as a region. Culture, history, economics, and race were integral elements for Key (1949), and these still play a role in the 21st century. Moreover, race still plays a central role in the politics of the South (see Aistrup, 2010, 2011), even nearly 60 years after the Civil Rights Act and nearly 70 years after the *Brown v. Board of Education* decision. Although the South may be distinct, the differences are not static – they change over time. Indeed, depending on the factors one examines, the South may be thought of as less distinct (Steed et al., 1990) and, paradoxically, more distinct (Travis et al., 2016). The result is a patchwork of changing dynamics.

There are two schools of thought regarding change in the South. On the one hand, the migration of people from the "Rust Belt" states to the southern states has been an ongoing process; the population of the South has grown steadily as the populations of states in the Northeast and Midwest have shrunk. This in-migration, argue some, has the effect of diluting both southern culture and long-standing political uniqueness (see Hillygus et al., 2017; Hood & McKee, 2010). The net effect of this change is that the South has lost its uniqueness and become much more like the rest of the nation in political terms. Whereas the South was once a bastion of conservatism, the result is a move toward the liberal end of the scale, particularly in the "Rim South" states.[2] However, the available evidence on this point is, at best, muddled.

A competing school of thought suggests that the South has actually become a national political trendsetter (Appelbome, 1996). This argument suggests that the electoral trends prevalent in the South for generations have been spreading to states outside the South, and that politics across the United States exhibit features once thought to be unique to the South. In short, the South is not becoming like the rest of the nation; the rest of the nation is becoming more like the South (see Appelbome, 1996; Breaux et al., 1998). When one examines state policy choices, this school of thought is supported by empirical evidence. For example, Breaux et al. (1998) argued that Mississippi was the de facto model for the 1996 Temporary Assistance for Needy Families (TANF) law that allowed states to become much more restrictive with their welfare benefits. While this would suggest that the rest of the nation is becoming more like the South, the causality has not been firmly established. Additionally, if it is the case that the rest of the nation is becoming more like the South, then it is also likely the case that the South is becoming less distinct as a political region. A straightforward method to determine southern distinctiveness is to compare the policy choices of states in the South and non-South states, and to compare the factors that appear to drive policy choices in each group. To the extent that policy choices, or the drivers of policy, are different, we may conclude that the South also is distinct as a region.

What about Policy Outcomes?

The importance of state policy decisions and state policy action cannot be overstated. As practiced in the United States, federalism results in shared powers between the national, state, and local governments. While the nature of federalism has changed in practice over the years (see Kettl, 2020;

Wright, 1988), states have never lost their policy making power. In a "dual federalism" model (Wright, 1988), the national government and the states each maintain primary authority in their own unique policy spheres. In an overlapping model of federalism (Agranoff & Radin, 2015) the authority of the national government and states is intertwined, but there is still coordination in policy implementation (Burke, 2014). This is evident in the move toward the use of block grants in the 1980s, as evidenced by the Clean Water State Revolving Fund (CWSRF) and Law Enforcement Assistance Administration (LEAA) grants; with the added incentives of "progressive federalism" (see Gerken, 2014, 2017) during the Obama administration. In each of these models of federalism, state politics (and, therefore, state policy making) matters. States make policy decisions in the "lanes" within their policy authority, whether those decisions are completely within the realm of state authority (e.g., setting voter ID requirements; see Aistrup et al., 2019), or concern the state implementation of national policy (e.g., Medicaid expansion under the Affordable Care Act; see Morris et al., 2019). In either case, these state-level policy decisions have consequences for citizens, the state, and the nation.

While the politics of the South has been studied and cataloged by many, less attention has been paid to policy making in the South. Electoral outcomes are important in that they determine the composition of the formal policy makers – that is, the group with the most direct influence over the agenda-setting and policy adoption processes. If the outcomes of elections matter, then we would expect to see differences in the kinds and types of policies promulgated by formal policy makers. And, if the politics of the South are truly unique, then we would expect to see the policies adopted by southern states to be likewise distinct from those decisions made elsewhere.

The purpose of this volume is to examine the policy choices made by southern states, and to compare those choices to the choices made in non-southern states. We employ a range of policy arenas that have generated policy choices in all 50 states, and across which we have comparable (and adequate) data. Our approach is to employ a common set of explanatory variables for each policy arena, and then to add additional explanatory variables unique to that policy arena. Through this approach we are able to determine the relative importance of our base model in each policy arena, and to detect the relative importance of the model between southern and non-southern states.

Unlike "southern politics" (with its emphasis on electoral outcomes and partisan dimensions of rule), the literature on southern policy making and policy outcomes is somewhat less well developed. The extant literature, much of it written by the authors of this volume, indicate a decidedly mixed conclusion in terms of questions of southern distinctiveness. In some areas, the South can be shown to be uniquely different than other states, while in other policy arenas the differences are so slight as to be largely irrelevant. One of the reasons for the mixed findings is that the existing work has been conducted over a period of nearly 30 years. Much has changed during that span, both in terms of politics and culture. Comparing the findings of a study in the early 1990s with a study in the 21st century becomes problematic. Likewise, these studies were conducted by employing a wide variety of techniques, variables, models, and datasets. Much of the early work was done using cross-sectional data, while later work has often tested and analyzed multiple state-years of data. Cross-sectional studies provide a useful glance at a limited slice in time but are limited in their explanatory power. Likewise, a dataset with 50 cases or observations provides limited degrees of freedom because of the "cases/variables problem" (Goggin, 1986), which further limits the explanatory power of the models.

In this book, we take a different approach to our analyses. First, we employ a standard set of explanatory models across all of our policy arenas. This allows us to not only determine whether there is a common set of important variables across all our policy arenas but also to determine the relative importance of each of our explanations. For example, if our political variables are consistently significant across our policy arenas, we might conclude that politics matters as an explanation of policy outcomes. Second, if politics matters in only a few policy arenas but sociodemographic or explanations of need are significant in all the models, we might conclude that political explanations are more important. The contribution of this book is to examine the efficacy of these different explanations across a set of policy arenas and decisions, which in turn allows not only to test for differences between southern and non-southern states but also to detect the most important explanators of policy outcomes in southern states. Through this process we may develop a deeper understanding of the degree to which distinctiveness in politics in the South leads to unique patterns in policy outcomes. This process, in turn, allows us to examine questions of southern distinctiveness, and to determine whether the South is becoming more or less distinct.

Layout of the Book

This book is divided effectively into three parts. The first part lays out an argument for southern distinctiveness; the second part provides empirical tests for distinctiveness; and the final part seeks to provide an overall assessment of the distinctiveness of southern policy making. In the first part, evidenced by this chapter and Chapter 2, we present an argument for southern distinctiveness. In particular, Chapter 2 starts with a fundamental, but critical question: how do we define "South?" As we will see, this is a question of no small importance. This chapter also presents a brief history of the South as a region.

The middle part of the book focuses on our empirical evidence. Chapter 3 presents a model of policy making to be applied in the following analytical chapters. Because the same model will be applied to a series of different dependent variables covering different policy areas, this chapter provides the justification for the included independent variables and describes the potential explanatory power for each model (and each variable in each model to be tested). This chapter also provides a short description of the data and methods to be employed in the analytical chapters.

Our basic model of state policy making includes variables grouped into three separate explanations. The first model is a political explanation and seeks to test the significance of a set of political variables often found in the state comparative literature. These variables include party control of the legislature, party control of the governor's office, and state ideology. Since policy making is inherently a political process, we expect to find support for this explanation. Our second model is a socioeconomic model and includes measures of minority population, poverty rate, and unemployment rate. The third explanation is grounded in state need in the specific policy arena under examination; this model is discussed in more detail in the following.

Chapters 4 through 9 present a series of policy areas for analysis. Each chapter begins with a short background on the specific policy area and is followed by a detailed description of the dependent variables to be tested in the chapter. We have chosen the topics of each chapter to provide a cross-section of different policy arenas. For each policy area, we also present a set of independent variables unique to each arena. These variables may be thought of as indicators of policy need. For example, if we are discussing a state's choice whether to expand Medicaid coverage under the Affordable Care Act (ACA), we might measure state need by including the number of uninsured citizens in the state. Another useful measure might be a measure of health outcomes in a state. States with a higher incidence of obesity, heart disease, and cancer, for example, might have a greater need for health care coverage than a state in which citizens are generally healthier. This approach assumes that states make policy choices based on a perceived problem in the state, and they desire to address that problem through public policy (see Kingdon, 1995).[3] Each chapter applies the generalized model to the policy area, including the unique measures of need, and then discusses the findings of the analysis. Our policy arenas include firearm legislation, fatal police encounters, COVID-19 response, implementation of the Affordable Care Act, state responses to wastewater treatment requirements, and the availability of reproductive health services for women. Taken together, these policy arenas account for a mix of state policy authorities (e.g., reproductive rights for women, fatal police encounters, and firearm legislation), along with a mix of policies that represent state policy decisions within a framework of state implementation of federal policy (ACA implementation and wastewater funding decisions). The final analytical chapter examines state actions in response to the novel coronavirus pandemic. In this chapter, we compare the state decisions and actions regarding stay-at-home orders, school closures, restrictions on public gatherings, testing efforts, and decisions to lift closures and stay-at-home orders. We still employ a comparison of southern states to the rest of the nation, but because of the compressed time frame of these actions, we treat this chapter somewhat differently than the other analytical chapters.

The final chapter in this volume compares findings across the different policy areas and draws comparisons and contrasts across those areas. The chapter then addresses the underlying question of southern distinctiveness and the implications for our findings. We conclude with some thoughts regarding the future of the study of southern politics and policy making.

In sum, if southern politics matters, then state policy choices in southern states should be different than states outside the South. The next chapter addresses the question of how the "South" is defined and operationalized, and why our definition of the South makes a difference.

Notes

1 Most of the work in these latter two areas is to be found in studies of individual states, and/or histories of individual states. See, for example, Krane and Shaffer (1992) or Edgar (1998).

2 Scholars of southern politics often make a distinction between states of the "Deep South" and the "Rim South." The "Rim South" are states who share borders with non-South states, while "Deep South" states are those whose borders only touch other southern states. The "Rim South" is often defined as Virginia, Tennessee, Arkansas, Texas, and Florida. Although Florida technically does not meet the geographic definition of a "Rim State," scholars argue that long-standing in-migration to Florida from the Northeast and Midwest, coupled with immigration from the Caribbean and South America, particularly in South Florida, give Florida a political character that is much more in line with other "Rim States" than with states of the "Deep South." See McKee (2010) and Black and Black (1987) for arguments in favor of the "Two Souths" dichotomy; see Knuckey (2017) and Shafer and Johnson (2006) for arguments against the dichotomy.

3 There is a substantial literature that describes the policy process. Kingdon (1995) captures the link between policy problem and policy solution within his "multiple stream" framework, and provides a useful way to consider policy-making as a reactive process guided by identified problems.

References

Acharya, A., Blackwell, M., & Sen, M. (2018). *Deep roots: How slavery still shapes southern politics*. Princeton University Press.

Agranoff, R., & Radin, B.A. (2015). Deil Wright's overlapping model of intergovernmental relations: The basis for contemporary intergovernmental relationships. *Publius: The Journal of Federalism, 45*(1), 139–159.

Aistrup, J. (2010). Southern political exceptionalism? Presidential voting in the South and Non-South. *Social Science Quarterly, 91*(4), 906–927.

Aistrup, J. (2011). Racism, resentment and regionalism: The South and the nation in the 2008 presidential election. *American Review of Politics, 32* (Summer), 131–154.

Aistrup, J., Breaux, D., Hale, K., Morris, J.C., & Travis, R. (2019). Voter photo ID laws in the US: Back to the southern dummy variable. Paper presented at the Annual Meetings of the Southern Political Science Association, Austin, TX, (January).

Aldrich, J., & Griffin, J. (2017). *Why parties matter: Political competition and democracy in the American South*. University of Chicago Press.

Appelbome, P. (1996). *Dixie rising: How the South is shaping American values, politics, and culture*. Harcourt & Brace.

Baker, T., Steed, R.P., & Moreland, L. (Eds.). (1983). *Religion and politics in the South*. Praeger.

Bass, J., & DeVries, W. (1995). *The transformation of southern politics: social change and political consequences since 1945*. University of Georgia Press.

Black, E., & Black, M. (1987). *Politics and society in the South*. Harvard University Press.

Black, E., & Black, M. (1992). *The vital South: How presidents are elected*. Harvard University Press.

Breaux, D., Duncan, C., Keller, C.D., & Morris, J.C. (1998). Blazing the TANF trail: The southern mind and the politics of welfare reform in Mississippi. *American Review of Politics, 19*(Spring), 175–189.

Bullock, C.S., III (2010). *Redistricting: The most political activity in America*. Rowman & Littlefield.

Burke, B. (2014). Understanding intergovernmental relations, twenty-five years hence. *State and Local Government Review, 46*(1), 63–76.

Campbell, B. (1977). Patterns of change in the partisan loyalties of native Southerners: 1952–1972. *Journal of Politics, 39*(3), 730–761.

Cooper, C.A., & Knotts, H.G. (2017). *The resilience of southern identity: Why the South still matters in the mind of its people*. University of North Carolina Press.

Edgar, W. (1998). *South Carolina: A history*. University of South Carolina Press.

Elazar, D.J. (1972). *American federalism: A view from the states* (2nd ed.). Thomas Crowell.

Gerken, H.K. (2017). Distinguished scholar in residence lecture: A user's guide to progressive federalism. *Hofstra Law Review, 45*(4), 1087–1096.

Gerken, H.K. (2014). Federalism as the new nationalism: An overview. *The Yale Law Journal, 123*(6), 1889–1918.

Goggin, M. (1986). The 'too many cases/too few variables' problem in implementation research. *Western Political Quarterly, 38*, 328–347.

Hillygus, D.S., Mckee, S., & Young, M. (2017). Reversal of fortune: The political behavior of white migrants to the South. *Presidential Studies Quarterly, 47*(2), 354–364.

Hood, M.V., III, & McKee, S. (2010). What made Carolina blue? In-migration and the 2008 North Carolina presidential vote. *American Politics Research, 38*(2), 266–302.

Kapeluck, B.D., Moreland, L., & Steed, R. (2009). *A paler shade of red: The 2008 presidential election in the South.* University of Arkansas Press.

Kettl, D.F. (2020). *The divided states of America: Why federalism doesn't work.* Princeton University Press.

Key, V.O. (1949). *Southern politics in state and nation.* University of Alabama Press.

Kingdon, J. (1995). *Agendas, alternatives, and public policies* (2nd ed.). Longman.

Knuckey, J. (2017). The myth of the "two Souths?" Racial resentment and white party identification in the Deep South and Rim South. *Social Science Quarterly, 98*(2), 728–749.

Krane, D., & Shaffer, S. (1992). *Mississippi government and politics: Modernizers and traditionalists.* University of Nebraska Press.

Levendusky, M. (2009). *The partisan sort: How liberals became Democrats and conservatives became Republicans.* University of Chicago Press.

Lublin, D. (2004). *The Republican South: Democratization and partisan change.* Princeton University Press.

McKee, S. (2010). *Republican ascendancy in southern U.S. House elections.* Westview Press.

McKee, S. (2019). *The dynamics of southern politics: Causes and consequences.* Sage.

Maxwell, A., & Shields, T. (2019). *The long southern strategy: How chasing white voters in the South changed American politics.* Oxford University Press.

Morris, J.C., Mayer, M., Kenter, R., & Lucero, L. (2019). *State politics and the Affordable Care Act: Choices and decisions.* Routledge.

Nadeu, R., & Stanley, H.W. (1993). Class polarization in partisanship among native southern whites, 1952–90. *American Journal of Political Science, 37*(3), 900–919.

Reed, J.S. (1983). *Southerners: The social psychology of sectionalism.* University of North Carolina Press.

Shafer, B., & Johnston, R. (2006). *The end of southern exceptionalism: Class, race, and partisan change in the postwar South.* Harvard University Press.

Steed, R., Moreland, L., & Baker, T. (Eds.). (1990). *The disappearing South? Studies in regional change and continuity.* University of Alabama Press.

Travis, R., Morris, J.C., Mayer, M., Kenter, R., & Breaux, D. (2016). Explaining state differences in the implementation of the Affordable Care Act: A south/non-south comparison. *Social Science Quarterly, 97*(3), 573–587.

Wilson, C.R., & Ferris, W. (Eds.). (1989). *The encyclopedia of southern culture.* University of North Carolina Press.

Woodward, J.D. (2013). *The new southern politics* (2nd ed.). Lynn Reiner.

Wright, D.S. (1988). *Understanding intergovernmental relations* (3rd ed.). Brooks Cole Publishing.

2 Where Is the South?

Sectionalism in the United States has driven our history. The US Constitution, from its earliest drafts, reflected a sharp difference of both geography and behavior – resulting in both the creation of a Senate with real power, and the minutiae of elements such as the 3/5th clause to determine representation in the House. The 10th Amendment – wrapped in the sanctity of the Bill of Rights – is directly related to the fear that states headed in different directions ideologically, culturally, and economically, might lose all autonomy following that vast revision of the Articles of Confederation. The great sectional divide that separated the founders was precariously balanced on a central fulcrum, both economic and cultural: the use of human beings as agricultural machinery. V.O. Key (1949, p. 5) has said, properly, that "Whatever phase of the southern political process one seeks to understand, sooner or later the trail of inquiry leads to the [African American]."

The Europeans that would come to dominate the Americas would have to make a massive cognitive shift. All of the available land was owned in Europe, mostly by hereditary, aristocratic elites. Estates could be large (usually as the result of a law of primogenitor) or small (through partible inheritance) but every inch of land was owned – by someone or something (often the church[1]). Owning land in Europe resulted from inheritance; not purchase, nor the right of labor. Even in other colonial possessions – Clive's and Hastings' India, for example – the land was already developed, had to be wrested from the grip of its legal owners if it was to be had; and more to the point, few Europeans wanted to settle there permanently. Better the absentee landlord than the role of settler.

The American experience – on the east coast of the northern continent, at least – was quite different. If wealth was extracted in many colonial possessions, with the Europeans departing with full pockets, North American colonial intention was quite different. Not only was the land not yet given over to traditional agriculture, but the Europeans who came to the Americas planned to stay. This combination of factors precipitated the utter destruction

DOI: 10.4324/9781003134602-2

of the people already living there in tragically short order. After the indigenous people had been run off, killed, or otherwise forced out of possession, millions of acres of North America were there for the taking.

In "New England," as it came to be called, standard European small farming practices could be employed. The earth was rich, there was plenty of rainfall, and the crops suitable to create both subsidence and profit could be grown and harvested by a few people per farm. The draw of New England was a temperate climate, reasonable farming conditions, and rich, well-watered soil. Attracting immigrants was easy: it was a land of milk and honey to those denizens of the crowded slum-plots of London, Manchester, and Glasgow. They were enthusiastically willing to come and, once settled, to work – for and with – newer arrivals until they could find their feet and move farther west, to their own holdings.

The land to the south was hardly an attractive destination, for anyone. It was miserably hot and humid, near tropical, and had all the drawbacks of the tropics as well: yellow fever, malaria, blackwater fever, baked earth, and miserable swamps. There was an unrelenting parade of insects, snakes, and vermin. The crops that could grow – grow and turn a profit – required back-breaking labor and constant attention in these wretched conditions. Cutting cane in the swamps or picking cotton bolls in the shade-less furrows of a field shimmering in the heat was attractive to no one, no matter how desperate. There was no mechanical way to solve the problem; human drudgery was required.

The people who were forced to become the machines of southern industry were not laborers, nor workers, in anything approaching a normal sense: they were chattel property. They were forced onto ships in Africa, shipped like animals – hundreds of thousands died: shackled, thrown overboard, or simply starved to death on the way. Those that made it to the shores of the United States were sold into a mockery of life in which they became literal engines – appliances – of a brutal agricultural system that eventually stretched from the eastern shore of Virginia and North Carolina, to the swamps of Florida, to the plains of Texas. Resistance to the system was savagely met.

Slave owning was not a practice strictly defined by latitude. While not common in the northeast or the west, slavery existed in most of the colonies, and slaves were held in the majority of the new states when the Constitution was ratified. But it did not last for long in New England: slaveholding existed in Pennsylvania until 1780; New Hampshire and Massachusetts abolished slavery in 1783; Rhode Island and Connecticut in 1784. Vermont came in as a free state (Painter, 2006, pp. 70–72). Virginia and North Carolina both split, and their progeny, Kentucky (1792) and Tennessee (1796), were both slaveholding states. By 1820, with the addition of Louisiana (1812),

Mississippi (1817), Alabama (1819), and Missouri (1820) as slave states; Indiana (1816) and Illinois (1818) as free states, the numeric balance was met at 12 states each. The "balance" was maintained into 1837, with the addition of Arkansas (1836) as a slave state; Michigan came into the Union in 1837 as free. In 1845, Texas came in as a slave state – eastern Texas was plantation land – and Iowa's entry as a free state in 1846 produced a shaky equilibrium. But with the addition of new territories (New Mexico, Kansas, and Wisconsin) the balance began to break down. By 1858, Wisconsin (1848), California (1850), and Minnesota (1858) had come in as free states, and the stage was set for trouble.[2]

The division of the United States into two disparate and desperately different "sections" – North and South (for there as yet was no "West") – was defined by the institution of slavery. The preservation of this institution became the primary incentive to political action, the cause célèbre of all "Southerners" and the raison d'être of nearly every political undertaking for those politicians who hailed from slave states. The slave system permeated every aspect of life: color was everything, since the slaves were almost entirely natives of West Africa. It was absorbed by osmosis into the political system as well and not a single aspect of the political order of slave states was unaffected: the judiciary, the legislature (and legislation), statute, and implementing policy all turned on the ever-present institution of slave labor.

Given the sectional nature of slavery, this meant that southern states – and their governmental structures – were simply different from their northern (and, later, western) neighbors. In political outlook, the primacy of first the slave system, then after the Civil War, white supremacy, and the restoration and maintenance of antebellum plantation elites, guided every political battle, every statutory output. "Liberty" for most white Southerners turned on the concept that states were sovereign, with "liberty" to make their own policies, their own laws, and to self-govern in as close to complete autonomy as possible – all in order to maintain a system rapidly deplored elsewhere in the United States and therefore, viewed as constantly under threat from outside its confines.

"Democratic liberty exists solely because we have slaves … freedom is not possible without slavery," pronounced the Richmond *Enquirer* in 1856; John C. Calhoun, the "statesman" of slavery, pontificated: "The defense of human liberty against the aggressions of despotic power have been always the most efficient in States where domestic slavery was to prevail" (Jenkins, 1857, p. 453). This classic pretzel logic, today, seems ludicrous and massively self-contradictory – but it was a logic that was defended, embedded, and internalized in the South.

This is the logic of an entitled elite, whose definition of "liberty" referred to the static order; one in which all citizens knew their place and their notions of "defense" clearly referred to anything or anyone who sought to upset the settled order. In the American setting, this classically regressive form of political theory was in response to perceived exogenous threats from the federal authority, and endogenous threats from restive elements within. The tension in which state authority is held between these two poles produces systems and traditions of government that is more than usually resistant to changes of any sort. In the end, change itself can be viewed with hostility, whether or not it can be tied to actual perils of either sort.

Secession as a Dividing Line

Key (1949) uses secession as his great cleavage between southern states – the states he investigated – and non-southern states – those he did not. Recent attempts to add states using other dimensions usually direct us to such features as slaveholding, or the introduction or the presence of segregation laws. As seen above, slaveholding immediately after the Revolutionary War, could initially mean any state might possibly be included. But even confining ourselves to those which held slaves at the outbreak of hostilities, this would include Maryland, Delaware, Kentucky, and Missouri. There have also been attempts to include Oklahoma – which was not a state, but a territory, in 1860 (see Bullock & Rozell, 2014). The clear historical argument pushes slaveholding states into three descending categories: (1) states with slavery, but did not hold secession conventions; (2) states which held slaves and held a secession convention, but did not secede, and (3) states that held slaves, held a secession convention and actually seceded, joined the new Confederacy, and fought a war with the remaining states of the Union. We reason, as we believe did Key, that the degree of investment in the institution is a measure of the "southerness" of a state.

If the cause of the Civil War has become oddly ambiguous in the face of some revisionist histories, it was not obscure to those in the slave states who seceded from the Union and fought it. The entwining of slavery as an institution with some Southerner's notions of democratic government are plain. This assertion must be understood under the shared assumption by most Whites in the slave states at the time that slaves were not in any understood sense "human," and therefore were not included in the matrix of persons and institutions interacting as "free" – and that the direct and savage oppression on these chattels was not in any way to be interpreted as "despotic." As to slavery's role as a construct implicit in the survival of White society, the sense appears to be that the labor that led to its prosperity has to be performed by another – non-white, subhuman – agent. White supremacy and all that followed from it was not only held as matters of law, but as tenets of deeply held cultural and scientific "realities" rarely, if not wholly, unquestioned by the White polity.

Only about 25 percent of the White population of the seceding states owned slaves at all – and less than 1 percent held 50 or more. Further, the counties that had the greatest concentrations of slaves were themselves relatively concentrated geographically as well. The great question is, how were those Southerners with no direct investment in slavery persuaded to shed blood for the institution? The answer, of course, is that not all were. Though they might be racist – most Whites were, north and south – some were not easily hoodwinked into the idea that they should be willing to lay down their lives for the property and prosperity of others. A quick glance at the home counties for those voting against secession in the conventions – or the vote for Republicans in the election of 1860 – reveals a core of White people who were opposed to secession which can expressly be linked to their status as non-slaveholders (Wooster, 1958, pp. 360–368).

The converse is also true. There were 13 secession conventions linked to separation from the Union prior to the Civil War. Of these, 11 were successful in passing and enforcing an ordinance of secession.[3] Seven states seceded by February 1861 (South Carolina, Mississippi, Florida, Alabama, Georgia, Louisiana, and Texas); four more seceded following the fall of Fort Sumter and the call for troops to defend the Union which followed (Virginia, Arkansas, North Carolina, and Tennessee); four "border states" (Maryland, Delaware, Kentucky, and Missouri) never seceded (Cooper, 2011, p. 4).

The reason for designating the seceding states as the "South" is not slavery alone, but rather the high level of investment in that institution and all that it brought with it. The extent to which these states were willing to go to defend and protect it is clearly seen in the act of secession (and later, their armed rebellion). Under this standard, Maryland, Delaware, Kentucky, and Missouri never "qualified." Our reasoning, and we believe Key's, is that the level of support for the institution of slavery and its later manifestations in White supremacy led to the outputs of African-American voter exclusion, Jim Crow laws, and other segregation measures and was deeply twisted into the sociopolitical fabric of these states. The states that demurred fall into some other category.[4]

The logical chain seems clear to us. The institution of slavery gave rise to a deeply felt, but intentionally constructed brand of conservatism. State sovereignty is here tied explicitly to a virulent form of racism, both as a central construct and as the fulcrum for state's rights. This conservatism has outlived the institution it was created to rationalize and protect, and not unreasonably, it is most embedded in states where the institution was most radically defended. If the states that held succession conventions, but did not secede, might be considered "the *almost* South," then it is probably apt to draw into focus a subgroup of those that did secede. It is not odd, given our logic here, that the most recalcitrant in their conservatism of this peculiar southern type are the states that also held the most slaves, and whose economies were most dependent on the institution: the "Deep South" of South Carolina, Mississippi, Alabama, Georgia, and Louisiana. Within the larger group of southern states and in finer, comparative, terms Tennessee, Florida, Texas, Arkansas, North Carolina, and Virginia are often counted less "southern" (i.e., the "Rim South").

This measure manifests in partisanship as well: Key himself used partisan consistency as a measure for "southerness," noting, "the eleven states that meet the test of partisan consistency also are the eleven states that seceded to form the Confederacy" (Key, 1949, p. 11). Key's partisan consistency measure was drawn on the Democratic Party of the 1876–1944 period, and though the shift of the South to the Republican party in the intervening years rather confuses the issue today, a similar measure could be introduced which holds as well: using "those states that between 1944 and 2021 went from being wholly dominated by the Democratic party but switched in allegiance almost wholly to the Republican party" describes both the overall "South" as well as the subgroup. Where formerly solidly Democrat, the deepest red of the states today are the original "Deep South" states. The "border" or "Rim" South states are more malleable in their support for the Republican party than their "Deep South" neighbors.

"Conservatism," in the Burkean sense, is not only a system that preserves the status quo and resists change but is also reciprocal: a loss to the forces of reform will animate the forces of reaction to regenerate the prior form whenever possible. The agents of preservation and retention, coupled with a will to reestablishment, make for a system that will always recreate itself – or attempt to. The system that developed in the American South was one that required both force from without and reform from within to fray the edges of the mechanics of the ruling elites that Key (1949) so adroitly profiles. From without, there were structural attempts to alter the system (the 13th, 14th, and 15th Amendments to the Constitution), as well as massive statutory alterations (the Civil Rights Act of 1964 and the Voting Rights Act of 1965 – and all of the attendant revisions and case law that issued from them). From within, there were demands and political action for reform, primarily coming from African Americans demanding some semblance of equality in systemic terms and equity in terms of policy.

Much of southern conservatism seems to turn on the apprehension of a false dichotomy: that democracy, as described by Calhoun and his coreligionists, brings with it anarchy, a threat to their notion of liberty – and that the rule of an elite political class is far preferable to it. In addition to stating this last directly, the following quote also preserves the endogenous expectations of such a system:

"People do not understand liberty or majorities," he remarked.

The will of a majority is the will of a rabble. Progressive democracy is incompatible with liberty ... Democracy is leveling ... Anarchy is more to be dreaded than despotic power ... The best government is that which draws the least from people, and is scarcely felt, except to execute justice.

John C. Calhoun (Jenkins, 1857, p. 453)

While it would be disingenuous to pretend that nothing has changed since Calhoun's pronouncement, there are many things in these sentiments that endure in the political culture of the South, and that we assert may be discerned in the southern approach to policy making.

Decades of research have been employed in research into the changes in voter franchise, partisan change, and the revision and realignment of the party system of the South. Much of this work labors to explain why the Republicans of the 1990s, 2000s, and 2010s so closely resemble – in attitude, organization, recruitment, and the like – the Democrats of the 1920s and 1930s. As the ballet of party change went forward, a veneer of "two-party-ism" – the absence of which Key so eloquently argued as the cause of southern political immobility – also began to emerge. But the two-party system in most southern states (until relatively recently[5]) has been just that: a veneer. The countless factions, sub-factions, and warring neighbors that Key sought to chronicle, were unified by two critical elements in the 1870s–1950s: an unmovable conservatism that demanded to be left alone, and a seemingly ironclad connection to the national Democratic Party, which promised to do exactly that, in return for a free hand in presidential elections. This critical tie began to fray after World War II, as the national Democratic Party began to make moves to interfere with the *status quo ante* of the cultural arrangements of the South (and political features which supported them). Southerners first moved to establish their own regionally distinct version of the Democratic Party[6] (The "Dixiecrats" – a miserable failure) and finally to begin to move to the GOP – albeit with fits and starts; "percolating downwards," in Bullock's famous phrase, from statewide office to state legislative districts (Bullock, 1988, p. 570). Essentially, Democrats became Republicans without really losing their basic political ideology, identity, or even factional alliances.

Despite the changes in partisanship and the expansion of the electoral franchise, there is an almost hypnotic correspondence in political attitude that permeates and continues to pervade the region. This is a spirit of aggressive resistance to governmental expansion (and the increased dedicated services that are coupled with it[7]) a hatred of taxing private wealth, generally; an apparent abhorrence to fund public collective goods, and an unwavering refusal to make changes in either the mechanics of their system or their general cultural orientation.

The South continues to be "The South." The 11 states which originally formed the Confederacy, through their shared history and the cultural orientation manifested from this history, continue to be guided in policy and politics by these features. As a result, the politics and policies resulting are measurably distinct from the rest of the United States, and the direct, as well as subtle effects of this will be revealed by the empirical examination that follows. The enduring question is not "is the South different," but rather "in what ways is the South *still* different?"

Notes

1 It likely did not escape the view of the founders that the European Church was often the largest landowner – even in Britain, where Henry VIII and his descendants disfranchised much church property, and it was remitted to the Crown.

2 On one hand, Oregon came in as "free" in 1858; but Oregon was a long, long way geographically from the center of what was increasingly identified as the slave "region." The Kansas territory, on the other hand, bordered directly on Missouri, a slavery bastion. The political issue, of course, was the balance of power in the Senate – when California came in as a free state, they sent one pro-slavery and one anti-slavery Senator to the chamber. By the late 1850s, save some hare-brained schemes to annex Northern Mexico or Cuba, there were essentially no more slave states to be "created." Fighting broke out between Kansas "Free-Staters" and proponents of the extension of slavery who came to be known as "Border Ruffians," resulting in several bloody clashes, including the firing and destruction of "Free State" newspaper offices and some other buildings in Lawrence, Kansas, as early as 1856.

3 Missouri's ordinance passed but was passed by a "rump legislature" and had no legal effect. Kentucky's elected government initially pursued a policy of neutrality, but a Confederate faction passed an ordinance of secession and the state was largely divided during the war. Due to the passage of the ordinance, Kentucky was accepted into the Confederacy. When Union troops drove the Confederates who held the Cumberland into Tennessee, Kentucky's status as a Union state was fait accompli. Both Missouri and Kentucky contributed troops to both the Union and Confederate armed forces.

4 For all of its issues as a territory, Oklahoma was still a territory, with a basically "western" history bound up in the issues concerning indigenous peoples. As with other conservative states, Oklahoma may have some shared values with the South, but is not, itself, a southern state.

5 The realignments of both Virginia (over the past decade) and to a degree, Georgia (in the 2020 presidential and 2021 senatorial elections) are both "legitimate"

realignments in that they mark a change not only in party, but in policy orientation. In the first perhaps due to the in-migration of government workers in the "crescent" of Northern Virginia and in the eruption of suburban progressive preferences and increasing African-American voting turnout.

6 A reemergence of this took place in 1968 and 1972, when George Wallace, the segregationist/racist traditionalist Governor of Alabama ran first as a third-party candidate (The American Party, a redux in many ways of the "Dixiecrats") in 1968, and then returned to the fold – sort of – of the Democratic Party to try an end-run around a clouded and heavily populated primary field as an outsider candidate "more Nixon than Nixon." Both efforts failed, but not before igniting real fear among party regulars, along with primary wins for Wallace in 1972 in Florida, Maryland, North Carolina, Tennessee, and Michigan.

7 Then Governor Rick Scott, of Florida, in his first term, refused to accept federal aid for light rail which several successive administrations had sought, arguing that private enterprise would provide the capital and partner with the state in its development. During the recent COVID-19 crisis, the Biden administration passed a relief/stimulus bill that would provide not only support for unemployed persons, but aid to states. Florida had been differentially hit hard by the crisis, as it did not have an income tax, and relied heavily on tourism taxes and income for general operations. Though the new governor accepted the funds with alacrity, now-Senator Scott urged the state to "give it back." It may be of some note that the state saw to use the windfall as a way to provide a tax cut for businesses.

References

Bullock, C. (1988). Regional realignment from an officeholding perspective. *Journal of Politics, 50*(3), 553–574.

Bullock, C., & Rozell, M. (Eds.). (2014). *The new politics of the old South: An introduction to southern politics* (5th ed.). Rowman and Littlefield.

Cooper, W. (2011). The critical signpost on the journey toward secession. *Journal of Southern History, 77*(1), 3–16.

Jenkins, J. (1857). *The life of John Caldwell Calhoun*. Alden and Beardsley. https://babel.hathitrust.org/cgi/pt?id=yale.39002006708680&view=1up&seq=463

Key, V.O. (1949). *Southern politics in state and nation*. University of Tennessee Press.

Painter, N. (2006). *Creating Black Americans: African-American history and its meanings, 1619 to the present* (pp. 70–72). Oxford University Press.

Wooster, R. (1958). An analysis of the membership of secession conventions in the Lower South. *Journal of Southern History, 24*(3), 360–368.

3 Model and Methods

Southern politics, identity, and culture have been studied extensively now for more than 70 years. And while labels have changed, and populations have shifted, there remains a general prevailing culture that permeates much of the region and influences decision-making and state action. In examining southern policy making, this chapter attempts to define boundaries within which to analyze several critical policy arenas, allowing for comparison and analysis about how and why the South acts in the manner it does across multiple policy domains.

To analyze policy making in the region, several key steps have been taken. The first is to review the relevant southern politics and state decision-making literature to identify a baseline model of state decision-making that frames and structures the analysis. There is natural variance between policy domains, but in general this includes political variables, socioeconomic variables, and policy need variables. The political and socioeconomic variables are mostly static across policy domains, while the need variables are unique to each included policy area.

The political variables include party control of the governorship, party control of the legislature, and prevailing citizen ideology within the state. The socioeconomic variables include state poverty level and minority population percentage. Need variables vary by policy domain and action. The areas of study include firearm legislation and restrictiveness, state implementation of the Affordable Care Act, reproductive rights for women, water quality standards, police violence, and pandemic response efforts. The selection of subject areas is due primarily to recent topical relevance: within each of these domains there have been wide-ranging impactful decisions and legislation in recent years, much of which is still ongoing. By analyzing decision-making across the six domains, we can build on the established work of southern politics, identity, and culture studies, and begin to unravel the thread of southern policy making; whether it is as unique as the region's politics, how or if it differs from the rest of the country, and why this may be.

DOI: 10.4324/9781003134602-3

What are the common "intangibles" that influence southern policymaking, and do they apply consistently across multiple domains; does the exercise support the theory of southern distinctiveness? The remainder of this chapter will discuss the roadmap for how we intend to address these issues: First, by discussing the factors influencing state decision-making, next by explaining the model specification and analytical technique, and finally by expanding on the data collection, sources, and potential limitations of our approach.

Political and Socioeconomic Factors Influencing State Decision-Making

This book seeks to better understand what drives southern policy making and whether it differs from the rest of the country; in short, to uncover the South's distinctiveness in terms of policy making, and to determine whether it differs across policy domains, and if it does, what factors drive policy making that differentiate it from the rest of the country. To begin to unravel these questions we first need to define the South. In this analysis, we do so by utilizing V.O. Key's (1949) conception of the South as the eleven Confederate States, including Alabama, Arkansas, Florida, Georgia, Louisiana, Mississippi, North Carolina, South Carolina, Tennessee, Texas, and Virginia. We then identify several key policy domains that have experienced substantial legislation, policy, and legal challenges in recent years. In nearly every case, we create index-dependent variables to measure policy restrictiveness to determine what factors predict support and opposition across policy domains and within and outside of the South.

This is done by developing a three-pronged model that examines political, socioeconomic, and need factors across the analyzed policy domains. Each policy domain is inherently different, and the models are structured as such, but the creation of a base model allows for cross-policy comparison and analysis to see specifically where factors influence or fail to influence policy creation. In addition to the political and socioeconomic models, each policy domain includes several "need" variables identified from the literature. A more complete discussion of political and socioeconomic factors follows below, while discussion of need variables will take place in each specific policy domain chapter.

Political Factors

Party Control of Governor

As the chief executive, the governor wields substantial power in state policy, direction, and decision-making. Across the nation, this impact can vary depending on the lens through which it is examined, and the powers granted to the office from state to state. In presidential elections, the governor's party affiliation has been found to have minimal correlation to state voting patterns (Erikson et al., 2012). The results are similarly inconclusive when attempting to identify the governor's party's influence on legislative voting behavior (Canfield-Davis et al., 2010). Across the nation, the governorship rarely has an impact on policy, independent of legislative control. Within the South, the results are more difficult to tease out due to a lack of variation: most southern states have and have had Republican leadership over the past three decades (Caughey et al., 2017). Generally, an issue must be of specific political interest to the governor for the party affiliation to correlate with policy outcomes (Bernick, 1978). When such an issue arises, the governor expends added political capital to ensure the desired outcome. Interestingly, when one begins to parse out southern states, one finds several examples of partisanship driving policy outcomes from the governor's mansion (Morris et al., 2019).

Party Control of Legislature

Legislative control has long been found to influence state policy making through agenda setting and dictating the policy process (Coleman-Battista & Richman, 2011; Cox et al., 2010; Hayes-Clark, 2012). A primary result of legislative control is the ability to direct and divert funding to majority interests (Brown, 1995). The party in power effectively controls the agenda and the purse strings through the legislative process. Unsurprisingly, the state policy process is far from neutral; politics and ideology play a substantial role. Democratic-controlled legislatures have been found to fund more extensive welfare and safety net programs, while their Republican counterparts often favor fewer tax-supported programs (Kousser, 2002). Like several other areas, the South is unique in this regard. A Democratic stronghold following the Civil War, the "solid South" was overwhelmingly controlled by White voters until the Civil Rights legislation in the 1960s. Almost overnight voting patterns changed from Democratic to Republican in presidential elections, but it was not until the early 1990s that congressional control in the South became almost uniformly majority – Republican (McKee, 2018).

Most studies that examine the influence of state legislature control on policy making approach it empirically from a 50-state model. However, when examined regionally, the results point to Republican partisanship being more fiscally stringent. Within the South, control of the legislature has been found positively to influence policy adoption in several varied models (Bentele & O'Brien, 2013; Haeder & Weimer, 2015), and Republican control has been shown to stall progressive policy proposals (Haeder &Weimer, 2015; Hale & McNeal, 2010). The difference is in the general lack of variation when examining the South independently from the rest of the country. Republican control of the legislature in the South is often far more of a deterrent for the progressive national policy agenda than it is in other areas of the country (Valentino & Sears, 2005). In addition to examining Republican legislative control, preliminary models were also run with percent control and unified party control. In each instance, there was little substantive difference with models yielding similar to lesser predictive power, resulting in the decision to focus on legislative control broadly.

Citizen Ideology

Citizen ideology has been found to be a strong predictor of state policy decisions, yet there are often challenges separating citizen ideology and party control of the legislature, which can be highly correlated (Berry & Berry, 1992; Breaux et al., 2007; Kim et al., 2010; and Soss et al., 2001). The issue of correlation between ideology and legislative control is not a new one and something that should not be unexpected. Berry et al. (1998) argue that a state legislature is effectively a collection of citizens, who are elected to represent (and in many cases mirror) the political ideology of their constituents. Thus, correlation is not only difficult to address but should be expected given the dynamics of political representation.

The ideological and party control similarities are not unique to the South, but the ideological leanings exhibit other regional differences rarely found elsewhere. Throughout much of the country, ideology refers to placement along a conservative/liberal spectrum of political thought (Scher, 2015). In the South, historically, citizen ideology has been deeply conservative and is often rooted in the politics of race and poverty (Scher, 2015). Citizen ideology is measured on a liberal–conservative continuum based on voter and candidate preferences in congressional elections. The unweighted average of scores represents state citizen ideology, with higher scores indicating a more liberal populace, and lower scores a more conservative one.

Socioeconomic Variables

Poverty

Poverty is an oft-cited driver of innumerable social ills and subsequently many policy attempts aimed at addressing such issues. Poverty affects individuals, community, opportunity, and policy matters. Poverty in the South has historically been about the ills of slavery, the exploited populations, and the ongoing malfeasance of Jim Crow and agrarian politics (McKee, 2019). The Civil Rights Act and the Great Society programs of the 1960s attempted to address racial injustice, poverty, and discrimination wrought by the region's "uniquely un-American experience with poverty, failure and defeat, guilt, and the pervasive fear of abstraction" (Bartley and Davis-Graham, 2019, p. 21).

As a region, the South remains the most impoverished area in the country, with approximately 44 percent of the nation's poor residing in the South (US Census Bureau, 2019). The impact of such widespread poverty has profound impacts on both community and policy. Poverty frequently leads to social exclusion, and the greater poverty and exclusion, the greater societal risk and impact (Wilkinson & Marmot, 2003). Fundamentally, the issue and impact of poverty is one of the resources. Impoverished individuals lack the resources to address basic needs, which is often where policy making comes in. Thus, one would expect areas with high concentrations of poverty would have a greater societal welfare need and more progressive policies to address such issues. This is not always the case, as welfare programs have been underfunded, incompatible with the issues, and culturally insensitive (Scher, 2015). To measure poverty, we employ state poverty rates and projections from the American Community Survey; this specifically captures the percentage of households below the federal poverty line.

Minority Population

Minority populations in the South have been exploited, attacked, and leveraged in countless political campaigns over the past century. From the overt racism of Jim Crow to the struggle for equal rights that culminated in protests, assassinations, and ultimately the Civil Rights Act, to more recent examples of high-profile minority candidates being elected to office, race has been an enduring political issue in the South. The influence and impact of minority populations in the South have long been a hallmark of southern distinctiveness. Traditionally, at least since the Civil Rights Era, the primary Republican strategy has been to pack large numbers of minority voters into a smaller number of districts, an electoral strategy designed to weaken minority voting strength (Hood & McKee, 2018). This maneuver has been met with disdain in the courts, where there has been some effort to promote minority representation, often through the creation of single-member districts (Scher, 2015).

These efforts have led to marked improvement of minority representation in positions of political leadership over the past three decades (Frederick, 2017). Greater representation and increasing diversity, as Latinos have become the fastest-growing minority in the South (McKee,

2019), have led to changing political dynamics throughout the region, especially in Texas and Florida. These rapidly changing minority population dynamics, along with increases in minority leadership, have found minority populations in the South with greater diversity and representation than in much of the recent past. The minority population is measured as the total and projected totals of state minority population as per the American Community Survey.

Need Variables

The included need variables vary by policy domain and in certain cases within policy domains by model. The inclusion of such variables is derived from the relevant literature of the six analyzed policy areas to allow for baseline comparison across models, while still accounting for key indicators, variance, and model specification concerns within each unique policy domain. The inclusion of need variables in each unique policy area is context specific and the discussion of these specific variables can be found in each individual chapter.

Model Specification and Analytical Technique

This book examines southern policy making and the political, socioeconomic, and need factors that influence and differentiate the South from the rest of the country. By selecting six disparate, but vast policy domains, and utilizing a previously developed framework (Travis et al., 2016) to guide the data collection and analysis; this work highlights and explains the complexity and trendlines that differentiate the South across policy domain and region from the rest of the country. The political and socioeconomic variables of the framework, along with the case-specific need variables provide a map through which to analyze and understand southern policy making and how it differs from the non-South.

The comparative policy domain approach allows for an in-depth examination of the decision-making processes within the 50 states by policy domain. This approach is further parsed to examine the decision-making drivers within the country, the South exclusively, and the remaining non-South states. This allows for insight and comparison in attempting to derive what drives southern policy making, whether it is unique across a series of predictors, and whether the characteristics vary by region and domain. The design, examining three models across each policy arena further highlights the complexities, challenges, and contrast that exist within and across the South and in contrast to the rest of the country and how those factors ultimately influence state decision-making to support or oppose the policies.

By examining several years of data, this study offers generalizable and invaluable insight into southern policy making and the context and trends that differentiate the decision-making process from the rest of the county. We are better able to understand the drivers of state and regional decision-making and how contextual and divergent it may be within and outside of the American South. In addition to the ability to better understand the regional dynamics discussed above, this analysis offers insight into the challenges of national legislation being implemented across the states, as is the case with each policy domain. Examining policy support and opposition in the context of political climate, socioeconomic factors, and contextual need provides evidence as to why southern states choose to support or oppose various legislative policies.

Dependent Variables and the Six Policy Domains

Each unique policy domain is characterized by a measure of support or opposition dependent variable.[1] In the majority of cases this measure is an index variable that measures state support and opposition to the given policy on an additive scale. Specific details and metrics will be discussed within each policy chapter but the general format across all chapters for the dependent variable remains the same. Each policy domain utilizes a multi-component dependent variable index that addresses state action related to a particular policy arena. Policy support is characterized by several critical decisions that are scored in support or opposition of each individual policy. Being an additive index, if states pursue a supportive action, such as adopting supportive auxiliary legislation, the state will receive a positive one score. An additional supportive action would result in a score of positive two, while a negative action, such as a lawsuit would shift the score back to a positive one. States receive positive or negative scores across each decision point that taken together indicate state support of opposition of a particular policy.

The six policy domains include firearm legislation and restrictiveness, state response to the Affordable Care Act, reproductive rights for women, water quality standards, police violence, and pandemic response efforts. Of the six, firearm legislation, the Affordable Care Act response, police violence, and pandemic response efforts utilize additive indices, while reproductive rights and water quality standards employ previously validated measures within their respective domains.

The base model predictors and restrictiveness indices afford substantial comparison and contrast, but there remain issues with the approach. We acknowledge that the different components of our dependent variable are likely viewed by state policy makers in different ways, and these decision-making points further vary from one policy domain to another. Some decisions may be rhetoric or nothing more than symbolic actions, while others may be viewed as more substantive in nature. Due to the nature of the study and analysis, focusing on state-level data, we cannot know the expected utility to any actor of a particular decision, or whether any actor views a specific choice as a symbolic or a substantive choice. We acknowledge that these actions might have different consequences but given the limitations of the data, we cannot examine or analyze these differences. Our dependent variable indices thus treat each element within the dependent variable policy domain equally. By examining state decision-making over the course of eight years, we are focusing on state/region response and action to policy.

Analytical Techniques

In order to test hypotheses across the six policy domains, we primarily employ ordinary least squares (OLS) regression analysis. Although several of the dependent variable indices can be viewed as categorical in nature, we utilize OLS[2] because we are treating the support and opposition measures equally. Further, additional testing using logistic regression models results in similar results to those reported in the following chapters. Thus, we are confident that the OLS results are not overly biased due to the limited range of the index-dependent variables. The data was imported into Stata/IC 16 for analysis. Prior to the analyses, the data were verified and checked for collinearity and heteroskedasticity across each model. Any known issues or concerns are discussed within each individual chapter. The subsequent chapters contain additional details that are policy domain specific to the unique models and analyses.

Each of the six analytical chapters includes descriptive statistics and at least three models, the baseline 50-state model, the non-South, and the South. In each case, except for Chapter 9, the data range is from 2012 to 2018 and includes sufficient observations for the modeling and analysis. Chapter 9, examining the initial state response to COVID-19, employs daily data from March 1, 2020, through July 31, 2020, to examine the initial five months, or first wave, of the state pandemic response. Chapter 9 includes several additional models and deviates the most significantly from the other analytical chapters given the data range, observations, and timeframe.

Data Collection

Data for our independent variables are drawn from a variety of sources, including the US Census Bureau, the US Department of Justice, the Kaiser

Family Foundation, *The New York Times*, the Sentencing Project, PoliData, the United Health Foundation, the American Community Survey, and Berry et al. (2010). Our data spans the years 2012 through 2018. The goal is to collect data uniformly across all states within the same time frame. The most recent (with the exception of COVID-19 response), major policy issue analyzed is the implementation of the Affordable Care Act (ACA). A starting point of 2012 allows us to capture the initial state decision-making of the ACA as well as each additional policy domain. The endpoint of 2018 is selected simply because that is the most recent year for which we are able to collect complete data sets across each policy area and variable. This seven-year period provides ample time and observations to analyze the models within each policy area, as well as contrast across policy domains. The data in this paper should be considered annual data, and not tied to a specific date during the calendar year.

Notes

1 Measuring restrictiveness or financial support.
2 Except in Chapter 9 where we run a series of logistic regression models to analyze the binary components of the index dependent variable individually.

References

Bartley, N., & Davis-Graham, H. (2019). *Southern politics and the second reconstruction*. JHU Press.

Bentele, K., & O'Brien, E. (2013). Jim Crow 2.0? Why states consider and adopt restrictive voter access policies. *Perspectives on Politics*, *11*, 1088–1116.

Bernick, L. (1978). The impact of U.S. Governors on party voting in one-party dominated legislatures. *Legislative Studies Quarterly*, *3*(3), 431–444.

Berry, F., & Berry, W. (1992). Tax innovation by American states: Capitalizing on political opportunity. *American Journal of Political Science*, *36*(3), 715–742.

Berry, W., Fording, R., Ringquist, E., Hanson, R., & Klarner, C. (2010). Measuring citizen and government ideology in the American States: A re-appraisal. *State Politics and Policy Quarterly*, *10*(2), 117–135.

Berry, W., Ringquist, E., Fording, R., & Hanson, R. (1998). Measuring citizen and government ideology in the American states, 1960–93. *American Journal of Political Science*, *42*(1), 327–348.

Breaux, D., Morris, J., & Travis, R. (2007). Explaining welfare benefits in the South: A regional analysis. *American Review of Politics*, *28*(1), 1–18.

Brown, R. (1995). Party cleavages and welfare effort in the American states. *American Political Science Review*, *89*(1), 23–33.

Canfield-Davis, K., Jain, S., Wattam, D., McMurtry, J., & Johnson, M. (2010). Factors of influence on legislative decision making: A descriptive study. *Journal of Legal, Ethical & Regulatory Issues*, *13*(2), 55–68.

Caughey, D., Xu, Y., & Warshaw, C. (2017). Incremental democracy: The policy effects of partisan control of state government. *The Journal of Politics*, *79*(4), 1342–1358.

Coleman-Battista, J.C., & Richman, J. (2011). Party pressure in the U.S. state legislatures. *Legislative Studies Quarterly*, *36*, 397–422.

Cox, G.W., Kousser, T., & McCubbins, M.D. (2010). Party power or preferences? Quasi-experimental evidence from the American states. *Journal of Politics*, *72*, 799–811.

Erikson, M., Folke, O. & Snyder Jr., J. (2012) A gubernatorial helping hand: How governors affect presidential elections. Research Institute of Industrial Economics. Stockholm, Sweden. http://hdl.handle.net/10419/81485.

Frederick, J. (2017). The persistent South: Southern distinctiveness, cultural identity, and change. 8th International Scientific Forum, ISF Proceedings.

Haeder, S., & Weimer, D. (2015). You can't make me do it, but I could be persuaded: A federalism perspective on the Affordable Care Act. *Journal of Health Politics, Policy and Law*, *40*(2), 281–323.

Hale, K., & McNeal, R. (2010). Election administration reform and state choice: Voter identification requirements and HAVA. *Policy Studies Journal*, *38*, 281–302.

Hayes-Clark, J. (2012). Examining parties as procedural cartels: Evidence from the U.S. states. *Legislative Studies Quarterly*, *37*(4), 491–507.

Hood, M.V., & McKee, S. (2018). Texas. In C. Bullock & M. Rozell (Eds.), *The new politics of the old south* (6th ed., pp. 302–337). Rowman & Littlefield.

Key, V.O. (1949). *Southern politics in state and nation*. Alfred A. Knopf.

Kim, H., Powell Jr, G., & Fording, R. (2010). Electoral systems, party systems, and ideological representation: an analysis of distortion in western democracies. *Comparative Politics*, *42*(2), 167–185.

Kousser, T. (2002). The politics of discretionary Medicaid spending, 1980–1993. *Journal of Health Politics, Policy and Law*, *27*(4), 639–671.

McKee, S.C. (2018). *Republican ascendancy in southern US House elections*. Routledge.

McKee, S. (2019). *The dynamics of southern politics: Causes and consequences*. CQ Press.

Morris, J., Mayer, M., Kenter, R., & Lucero, L. (2019). *State politics and the Affordable Care Act: Choices and decisions*. Routledge.

Scher, R. (2015). *Politics in the New South: Republicanism, race and leadership in the twentieth century*. ME Sharpe.

Soss, J., Schram, S., Vartanian, T., & O'Brien, E. (2001). Setting the terms of relief: Explaining state policy choices in the devolution revolution. *American Journal of Political Science*, *45*(2), 378–395.

Travis, R., Morris, J., Mayer, M., Kenter, R., & Breaux, D. (2016). Explaining state differences in the implementation of the Affordable Care Act: A South/non-South comparison. *Social Science Quarterly*, *97*(3), 573–587.

U.S. Census Bureau. (2019). Income and poverty in the United States: 2018. *American Community Survey*. https://www.census.gov/library/publications/2 019/demo/p60-266.html

Valentino, N., & Sears, D. (2005). Old times there are not forgotten: Race and partisan realignment in the contemporary South. *American Journal of Political Science, 49*(3), 672–688.

Wilkinson, R., & Marmot, M. (2003). *Social determinants of health: The solid facts* (2nd ed., pp. 1–32). World Health Organization, Europe.

4 Implementation of the Affordable Care Act

Perhaps no federal policy of the 21st century has been as contentious and politically charged as the Patient Protection and Affordable Care Act (or ACA; P.L. 111–148). Enacted in 2010 during President Barack Obama's first term in office, it represented the most sweeping reform of federal health care policy since the 1960s. The ACA consisted of a collection of policies designed to, among other goals, control healthcare costs, impose new efficiencies in the healthcare sector, and extend healthcare insurance coverage to a larger proportion of Americans. The two most controversial elements of the legislation were a requirement for Americans meeting certain criteria to purchase healthcare insurance in the private insurance market, and the expansion of the Medicaid program to include healthcare coverage to a larger share of low-income Americans. Implementation of the ACA began in earnest in late 2010, and implementation is ongoing. Several attempts to invalidate the ACA have been attempted over the years, and as of this writing in early 2021, the basic framework has remained.

The ACA was designed to give states a range of options in terms of implementation. Among other alternatives, states have the choice to create a state-run insurance exchange to provide insurance options to citizens; they can also default to a federally run insurance exchange. The law initially required all states to expand their Medicaid programs, but a later Supreme Court challenge allowed states to opt out of Medicaid expansion. States also could choose to oppose the ACA, as was the case for many Republican-led states. Similar to many federal policy initiatives, some states embraced the new law, while other states opposed it, either actively or passively. This chapter analyzes the initial implementation choices of states to determine whether southern states followed a different path toward implementation of (or a form of resistance to) the ACA. Did the policy responses of southern states differ from those of other states, or was the South indistinct from the rest of the nation? Because the implementation of the ACA took place in

DOI: 10.4324/9781003134602-4

a relatively compact period of time, our ability to compare across states is enhanced, in that it lessens the impact of changes over time.

The ACA provides a useful lens through which to compare the South to the rest of the nation for several reasons. First, previous research in the ACA (see Barrileaux & Rainey, 2014; Travis et al., 2016) indicates that state policy choices were not driven by policy need, but instead by partisan politics and ideological differences. This allows us to test the efficacy of these explanations, since the South tends to exhibit a reasonably high degree of homogeneity in terms of ideological orientation. Second, much of the scholarly work focused on the ACA tends to employ single measures of state action – the decision to expand Medicaid, for example. This chapter employs a dependent variable that captures a range of potential state actions in regard to ACA implementation. Third, the ACA represents a significant departure from previous iterations of national healthcare policy, and state decisions regarding program implementation have impacts that last well beyond initial program implementation. Finally, the question of southern distinctiveness is brought clearly into focus: do southern states remain analytically distinct from the rest of the nation? Are the choices of southern states collectively different from the decisions made by other states?

Elements of the Affordable Care Act

The Affordable Care Act was, arguably, the defining piece of federal legislation of the Obama presidency. Obama campaigned in 2007 on a promise of healthcare reform, and he exhorted Congress to take up the issue early in the legislative session. The initial discussion in Congress centered around a private insurance-based model first proposed in Massachusetts by then-Governor Mitt Romney, and Obama quickly threw his weight behind this policy model. The basic policy model combined an expansion of the use of privately held health insurance, along with a federal mandate to require those meeting certain income tests, and who did not receive employer-provided healthcare insurance, to purchase insurance through a government-sponsored market. This was to be combined with a mandate to states to expand their Medicaid programs to increase participation by low-income groups in the Medicaid program, and thus expand healthcare coverage to those Americans too wealthy to qualify for the then-current Medicaid program, but too poor to afford private insurance.

There were several factions in Congress that began to stake out different policy positions on the proposal. First, there was a group of mostly liberal Democrats who argued for a single-payer healthcare system (similar to Medicare), also known as "universal healthcare." This proposal was discussed widely, but never attracted a large coalition of supporters in

Congress. The second group was a larger group of moderate Democrats that supported some version of the Massachusetts plan that would rely on the private insurance market for coverage. Within this group were factions that wanted to combine the basic plan with a single-payer system; others that wanted just the basic plan; still others that wanted to combine the basic plan with Medicaid expansion; and several other variations of the same idea. Finally, Republicans opposed nearly all the options. Although there were several Republicans in each chamber that initially supported the basic plan, the Republican leadership in both chambers decided quickly that the best strategy was one of agenda denial. Republicans tried to derail the process with procedural votes, "poison-pill" amendments, and other tactics. After more than a year of often heated debate, the conference bill passed the House by seven votes; all Republicans and several Democrats voted against the bill. The bill was signed into law by President Obama on March 23, 2010.

It is reasonable to identify the individual mandate requirements in the bill as the most controversial element of the policy. The individual mandate requires all citizens not covered by employer-provided insurance, or who do not qualify for Medicaid, to purchase health insurance. A significant portion of the premiums are deductible for tax purposes, but citizens who do not participate are subject to a series of escalating tax penalties. The purpose of this framework was to ensure that there was ample incentive for the citizens targeted by these requirements to enter the insurance marketplace (Jeter, 2013; Kaiser Family Foundation, 2013a). Although citizens could purchase coverage as they saw fit, the law called for all states to create web-based health insurance exchanges in which citizens could be presented with a range of options and price points – in effect, a form of "one-stop shopping." The scheme also allowed for small businesses to purchase health plans for their employees at competitive rates (Kaiser Family Foundation, 2013a; Haeder & Weimer, 2013). In order to implement the state insurance exchange and aid in the growth of healthcare spending, the ACA required states to pass legislation to adopt certain market reforms.

In its original form, the ACA also tied continued federal funding for existing state Medicaid programs to the state decision to expand their Medicaid program to increase the number of citizens eligible for assistance. This provision quickly became a flashpoint for both governors and attorneys general in several states and led to a number of lawsuits challenging the constitutionality of the ACA. These cases were eventually consolidated into a single case, *National Federation of Independent Business v. Sebelius* (567 U.S. 519, 2012) when the Supreme Court granted it certiorari. Although the court reaffirmed the constitutionality of the law in a 5–4 decision, the court also ruled that states could not be coerced into accepting Medicaid expansion.

This decision essentially allowed states to choose whether or not they would expand Medicaid, removing the fear of the loss of Medicaid funding should they choose not to expand (Kaiser Family Foundation, 2013b). Three years later, in *King v. Burwell* (576 U.S. 473, 2015), the plaintiffs in that case asked the court to declare the entire law unconstitutional on the basis that the individual mandate was also coercive, and thus unconstitutional. However, in that case, the court ruled that the individual mandate was a form of a tax, and that Congress clearly had the right to levy taxes on individuals. The ACA thus survived two Supreme Court challenges. A number of executive orders during the Trump administration, coupled with a Republican-controlled Congress that removed the tax penalty for noncompliance further attempted to gut the legislation, but the program has endured. Arguments in yet another Supreme Court case were heard in October 2020. On his first day in office, President Biden vowed to sign executive orders to reverse many of the actions taken by the previous president to weaken the ACA (McIntire & Clason, 2021).

The removal of the requirement for Medicaid expansion has led to a great deal of uncertainty for low-income citizens whose incomes are too high to qualify for Medicaid: the so-called funding gap (Haeder & Weimer, 2013). This segment of the population tends to be the most vulnerable, and consists of low-income individuals, those with disabilities, minorities, and others (Kaiser Family Foundation, 2013c, 2013d, 2013e). Moreover, the effects of a decision to not expand Medicaid not only affects vulnerable citizens, it also negatively impacts hospital revenues, a particularly important issue in many regional health care networks (Holahan et al., 2013; Kaiser Family Foundation, 2013f).

States are thus faced with the requirement to make two core decisions related to the ACA: whether to institute a state-run insurance exchange, and whether to accept Medicaid expansion. Across the United States, states have taken different paths; some states have chosen to accept one or both of these responsibilities; others have actively opposed the law and its various requirements and benefits. Twenty-seven of the fifty states have either filed a lawsuit opposing the ACA or have joined an existing lawsuit. Initially, 23 states rejected Medicaid expansion, although several states have since accepted an expanded program. Furthermore, 21 states have passed state legislation in active opposition to the ACA and its implementation, the state laws range from resolutions of disapproval of the program to an outright rejection of the federal law.

Most existing research into state actions regarding ACA implementation have focused on explaining a single state choice; for example, whether a state is willing to accept Medicaid expansion (see, e.g., Barrileaux, 2013). Although some work has been done to take a more comprehensive view of state choice under the ACA (see, e.g., Travis et al., 2016; Morris et al., 2019, differences in action by states in the South as compared to the rest of the nation are largely unexplored. This chapter adopts the multifaceted measure of state action as developed by Travis et al., 2016), composed of an index of five possible state decisions and actions: the decision whether or not to adopt legislation requiring health insurance market reforms; whether to create a state-run health insurance market; whether the state has filed (or participated in) a lawsuit challenging the constitutionality of the ACA; whether a state has adopted Medicaid expansion; and whether a state has passed legislation in opposition to the ACA. The first two of these options indicate support for the ACA, while the decision to adopt Medicaid expansion can be construed as either supportive (adopt) or not (not adopt). The final two elements indicate active opposition to the ACA since both are designed to halt implementation.

A Model of ACA Implementation

Our dependent variable for this policy is the seven-point ordinal index created by Mayer et al. (2015) to measure the degree of acceptance or rejection of the ACA by a state. As stated above, some of the actions taken by states (e.g., adopting a state insurance exchange; passing market reform legislation; expanding Medicaid) are positive actions, while others (e.g., joining a lawsuit opposing the ACA or passing blocking legislation) are negative actions. For each of the three positive actions, states are awarded one point on the scale, and one point is deducted for each negative action. If a state chooses not to adopt Medicaid, a point is also deducted. Thus, a state that takes all three positive actions would receive a score of +3, while a state that took both negative actions and did not expand their Medicaid program would be scored as -3. It is clear that different possible actions are very likely to be interpreted differently by state decision-makers. For example, for a state to pass blocking legislation may be viewed by policy makers as a symbolic gesture, while a refusal to create a state-run insurance exchange may be a more substantive decision. However, because we are measuring the level of support at the state level, we cannot determine the intent of any specific policy maker or the expected utility of any single decision. We acknowledge the limitations of an approach that weighs all five decisions equally, but a more fine-grained distinction between actions is simply not possible. Table 4.1 presents descriptive statistics for the variables employed in this analysis.

Analysis

Table 4.2 highlights the analysis explaining state and regional decision-making related to health reform and the ACA. The initial, 50-state baseline

Table 4.1 Descriptive Statistics: ACA Implementation

	Obsv	Mean	Sd	Min	Max
Dependent variable	350	−.24	2.22	−3	3
Republican gubernatorial control	350	.62	.49	0	1
Republican legislative control	343	.59	.49	0	1
Citizen ideology	350	40.92	17.51	17.51	73.50
Poverty	350	10.27	2.84	4	19.20
Insurance	350	10.57	4.31	2.50	22.50
State health	350	.04	.51	−1.21	.99
South	350	.22	.41	0	1

Table 4.2 Regression Results: ACA Implementation

	Baseline Regression	Non-South	South
Republican gubernatorial control	.14	.14	.30
	(.21)	(.25)	(.50)
Republican legislative control	−1.49***	−1.38***	−3.13***
	(.22)	(.25)	(1.14)
Citizen ideology	.05***	.05***	.02
	(.01)	(.01)	(.02)
Poverty	.31***	.33***	−.04
	(.03)	(.04)	(.12)
Insurance	−.14***	−.15***	−.04
	(.02)	(.02)	(.05)
State health	.92***	1.08***	−1.36*
	(.19)	(.22)	(.72)
South	−.97***		
	(.16)		
Constant	−3.12***	−3.33***	.81
	(.68)	(.82)	(1.75)
Adjusted R^2	.80	.78	.33
N =	343	238	77

Note: Standard errors in parentheses. Levels of statistical significance: * 0.1; ** 0.05; *** 0.01. Bold coefficients indicate a significant difference at the 0.1 level in the effects for non-South versus South.

regression model explains 80 percent of the dependent variable index variance. That is, 80 percent of what has driven state decision-making toward health reform over the past decade. Examining this model, we find that each variable, except for Republican gubernatorial control to be highly predictive in explaining health reform. Republican legislative control, as expected, is a strong predictor of ACA opposition, much like a more liberal citizenry is a positive driver of health reform. These findings are generally as expected, with the exception of the uninsured rates. The baseline analysis shows greater uninsured rates across the states to have a negative relationship, effectively opposing health reform and the ACA. In this model, the South dummy variable is also significant.

Parsing out the southern states and looking exclusively at the 39 remaining non-South states, the relationship and directions of the analyzed variables remain largely static. However, when moving onto model three, examining only the southern states, we begin to see substantial variation across models. Unlike the first two models, the explained variance in the South is substantially less, indicating other factors, unmeasured in the prior models are driving decision-making. Still, Republican legislative control comes back as a strong negative predictor, highlighting ACA opposition in the South, much like across the rest of the country. The only other variable exhibiting any predictive significance within the South is state health, and surprisingly, or not, it is significant in the opposite direction as in the prior models.

Discussion/Conclusion

Examining the findings across models raises several interesting points. Across each model, it is not Republican governors driving the support or opposition to health reform, despite the front and center and outspoken approach that many Republican governors took during the initial implementation phase. In each case, Republican legislative control was significantly stronger in predicting ACA opposition. Much like Republican control, it is no surprise that uninsured rates are a significant predictor, but the direction comes as something of a shock. In the baseline and non-South models, states with greater populations of uninsured individuals were found to be significantly more likely to oppose health reform measures. The very populations the law was designed to aid, were some of the staunchest adversaries when it came to state support. A need measure, that perhaps highlights the deep partisan divides of this issue.

Exploring the models in unison on a case-by-case basis, it comes as little surprise that southern states are statistically significant in their opposition to the ACA. Many of these states were among those with the greatest rate of uninsured and poorest state health rates. Where this diverges however, is within the South-specific model. The strength of the model across the states and in the non-southern states is not reciprocated within the South. Many of the significant predictors across the prior models no longer retain significance. The only variable in congruence with the first two models is Republican legislative control as an impediment to health reform. Perhaps most startling is the change in direction of the health variable, indicating that across the country, healthier states were more likely to support health reform, yet in the South, where poor health is prevalent, such states were significantly more likely to oppose health reform measures.

What does it mean for the South and southern distinctiveness as it relates to health reform? The South is rather clearly distinct from the rest of the nation within this policy domain. The South is a significant predictor of opposition in the baseline model, despite several indicators of great need for improved health, access, and care. The obstructions in this case, Republican legislators, are not unique across regions, but what is, is the fact that need measures, and socio-demographic variables seemed to play little part in the early implementation period, especially in the South, where in at least one case, southern states went in the opposite direction as one would expect based on regional need.

It is important to note the difference in significant predictors and explained variance between the three models. The South is a significant predictor of ACA opposition, but for the most part, the model, which is overwhelmingly strong in explaining variance across the country and outside of the South, falls flat attempting to explain what is going on in Dixie. This revelation suggests, like others have before (see Elazar, 1984; Key, 1949), that there are other factors in play in the South. Culture, tradition, and moralistic leanings may have a greater influence in the South in terms of policy than elsewhere. These findings and their differences highlight the complexity and nuance in explaining policy making, and specifically, policy implementation in and across the South where need is not necessarily the primary driver of state decision-making.

References

Barrilleaux, C. (2013). The state politics of Medicaid expansion. Paper presented at the 13th State Politics and Policy Conference, May, Ames, IA.

Barrilleaux, C., & Rainey, C. (2014). The politics of need: Examining governors' decisions to oppose the 'Obamacare' Medicaid expansion. *State Politics and Policy Quarterly*, *14*(4), 437–460.

Elazar, D. (1984). *American federalism: A view from the states* (3rd ed.). Harper & Row.

Haeder, S., & Weimer, D. (2013). You can't make me do it: State implementation of insurance exchanges under the Affordable Care Act. *Public Administration Review*, *73*(s1), 1–14. http://www.healthypeople.gov/2020/topicsobjectives 2020/overview.aspx?topicid=39.

Holahan, J., Buettgens, M., & Dorn, S. (2013). The cost of not expanding Medicaid. In *Report: Kaiser Commission on Medicaid and the Uninsured*. Henry J. Kaiser Family Foundation.

Jeter, A. (2013). Pay for health insurance, or pay a tax penalty. *Virginian Pilot.* November 28. http://hamptonroads.com/2013/11/pay-health-insurance-or-pay-tax-penalty.

Kaiser Family Foundation. (2013a). Summary of the Affordable Care Act. In *Focus on health reform* (pp. 1–13). Henry J. Kaiser Family Foundation.

Kaiser Family Foundation. (2013b). What is Medicaid's impact on access to care, health outcomes, and quality of care? Setting the record straight on the evidence. In *Issue Brief: Kaiser Commission on Medicaid and the Uninsured* (pp. 1–13). Henry J. Kaiser Family Foundation.

Kaiser Family Foundation. (2013c). Faces of the Medicaid expansion: How obtaining Medicaid coverage impacts low-income adults. In *Kaiser Commission on Medicaid and the Uninsured* (pp. 1–28). Henry J. Kaiser Family Foundation.

Kaiser Family Foundation. (2013d). The impact of current state Medicaid expansion decisions on coverage by race and ethnicity. In *Issue brief: Kaiser Commission on Medicaid and the Uninsured* (pp. 1–10). Henry J. Kaiser Family Foundation.

Kaiser Family Foundation. (2013e). The impact of the Medicaid expansion for low-income communities of color across states. In *Key facts: Kaiser Commission on Medicaid and the Uninsured* (pp. 1–10). Henry J. Kaiser Family Foundation.

Kaiser Family Foundation. (2013f). Analyzing the impact of state Medicaid expansion decisions. In *Issue brief: Kaiser Commission on Medicaid and the Uninsured* (pp. 1–10). Henry J. Kaiser Family Foundation.

Key, V.O. (1949). *Southern politics in state and nation.* University of Alabama Press.

King v. Burwell. (2015). 576 U.S. 473.

Mayer, M., Kenter, R., & Morris, J. (2015). Partisan politics or public-health need? An empirical analysis of state choice during initial implementation of the Affordable Care Act. *Politics and the Life Sciences, 34*(2), 44–51.

Morris, J., Mayer, M., Kenter, R., & Lucero, L. (2019). *State politics and the Affordable Care Act: Choices and decisions.* Routledge.

McIntire, M.E., & Clason, L. (2021). Biden uses executive orders to address COVID-19, other health care issues. *Rollcall.com.* https://www.rollcall.com/2021/01/21/biden-uses-executive-orders-to-address-covid-19-other-health-care-issues/.

National Federation of Independent Business v. Sebelius. (2012). 567 U.S. 519.

Travis, R., Morris, J., Mayer, M., Kenter, R., & Breaux, D. (2016). Explaining state differences in the implementation of the Patient Protection and Affordable Care Act: A South/non-South comparison. *Social Science Quarterly, 97*(3), 573–587.

5 Reproductive Rights for Women

The issue of reproductive rights for women has been in the vanguard of major national policy issues for decades. Since the landmark 1973 Supreme Court decision in *Roe v. Wade*, the debate has been bitter, partisan, and sometimes violent as both states and the national government have tried to address the question of reproductive rights for women. The struggle in this policy domain can be construed as an attempt to define the rights that attach as a result of the *Roe* decision. More recently, however, the locus of the conflict has shifted from the national level to focus on the role of the states in reproductive rights policy.[1] Court cases such as *Planned Parenthood of Southeastern Pennsylvania v. Casey* (1992) and *Webster v. Reproductive Health Services* (1989) have served as the impetus to define a greater role for states in this policy arena. States have responded over the years in policy terms by enacting laws targeted at insurance coverage for contraception, parental or spousal notification, mandatory counseling, or mandatory waiting periods, among others. The trend in state policy activity in this arena is obvious: 15 states had parental notification laws on the books in 1991 (Oakley, 2003), but by 2005, 44 states had enacted some form of parental notification or consent law (NARAL, 2006). For example, in 2005 alone, state legislatures across the country debated over 600 separate bills intended to restrict female reproductive rights (NARAL, 2006).

Opposition to reproductive rights for women is a hallmark of some forms of socially conservative politics. Given the rampant conservatism of southern states, one might expect the South to be much more opposed to reproductive rights than other states. If Key (1949) is right in his assertion that the South is truly distinct, then we should be able to detect differences in state choices in reproductive rights policy, as have been detected in other policy arenas. On the other hand, the Catholic Church stands opposed to reproductive rights (particularly contraceptive devices and abortion), and Catholicism is most prevalent outside the South. Support for a null hypothesis might indicate that reproductive rights is an area that cuts across regional

DOI: 10.4324/9781003134602-5

distinctions, or it may indicate that the South is losing some of its distinctiveness (Aistrup, 2010; Buchanan, 2009), that the South is becoming more like the rest of the country, or that the rest of the country is becoming more like the South (see Appelbome, 1996; Breaux, et al., 2002).

A Model of State Choice in Reproductive Rights

While many studies focus specifically on access to abortion services (see Barkan, 2014; Hussey, 2010; Kreitzer, 2015; New, 2011), few scholars attempt to examine a broader range of reproductive rights policies. Several states enact policies that do not specifically address abortion but serve to limit access to reproductive care. In order to capture the broad range of state restrictiveness, we adopt the use of the NARAL Pro-Choice America Report Card (NARAL, 2012–18), as our dependent variable (see Appendix). The score for each state is derived by adding points for policies that restrict access to abortion and other reproductive services and subtracting points for laws that liberalize access to these services. The scores also account for the severity of the laws, as well as the degree to which a state actively enforces the relevant laws.

Although NARAL is clearly an advocacy group, their scoring system has been both examined and employed in previous academic literature (see Gohmann & Ohsfeldt, 1994; Haas-Wilson, 1996; Kahane, 1994; Medoff, 2002; Oakley, 2003; Wetstein & Albritton, 1995). Gohmann and Ohsfeldt (1994) compared NARAL's score with their own measure of abortion rights in an attempt to predict which states would be most likely to restrict abortion and found that the NARAL score correctly classified states 87 percent of the time, while their own measure was correct only 75 percent of the time.

Common Explanations in the Literature

A review of the extant literature reveals a wide range of variables previously employed in studies of abortion rights. Much of this work has focused on a narrow range of explanations. This section briefly reviews the extant literature and presents the variables to be added to our baseline model of state policy choice.

Factors such as increased wealth, greater population concentration, and diversity of race have shown to result in a more liberal policy culture. Previous research on abortion rights has linked a more liberal policy culture with lower levels of restrictiveness on abortion (Wetstein & Albritton, 1995). Strickland and Whicker (1992) suggest that the diversity typically found in urban areas would lead to pro-choice attitudes, while more homogeneity in rural areas would foster support for more restrictive policies. This finding is consistent with Hansen (1980), who found a positive relationship between the percentage of a state's population living in urban areas and less restrictive abortion policies. Given that the levels of urbanization in the South are not significantly different than those in the rest of the nation (taken as a whole), we would expect higher levels of urbanization in southern states to be negatively related to policy restrictiveness, but likely not at a statistically significant level.

In general, the extant literature supports the link between urbanization and policy liberalization. In addition to the diversity argument, there is research that reports a positive relationship between income levels and pro-choice attitudes (Strickland & Whicker, 1992). The well-established correlation between income and education would also suggest that populations with higher levels of education would be less supportive of restrictive policies. However, Jelen and Wilcox (2003) report a significant decline in the correlation between education and pro-choice attitudes during the 1990s, although the change was most notable among those who identified themselves as Republicans. While per capita income levels in southern states tend to lag behind those in other states, we would still expect higher per capita income to result in less restrictive reproductive policies.

Related to the issue of per capita income is the unemployment rate in a state. Unemployment rates fluctuate with economic growth; a strong economy places more pressure on labor markets, in turn placing pressure on states to reduce the number of people on public assistance and thus create more people in the labor force. Soss et al. (2001) hypothesized that states with lower unemployment rates would tend to favor more restrictive welfare policies, because of the greater pressures in the labor market for workers. We expect to see a similar relationship for the restrictiveness of reproductive rights.

The question of race and its effect on both attitudes on abortion and the restrictiveness of state policy are somewhat less clear. Statistics from the Centers for Disease Control (CDC, 2000) indicate that the majority of abortions were performed on White women (55 percent), while 35 percent were performed on Black women, and seven percent listed race as "other" (three percent were unreported). However, the abortion rate for Black women (31 per 1,000) was more than three times the rate for White women (10 per 1,000); for Hispanics the rate was 16 per 1,000 women. While White women are less likely to obtain an abortion, Strickler and Danigelis (2002) report generally greater support for abortion among White women. Strickland and Whicker (1992) find that the percentage of Blacks in the population is not a significant predictor of state restrictions on abortion, although states with larger Hispanic populations were likely to have less restrictive policies toward abortion. The findings regarding Hispanic populations were also supported by New (2014). This may suggest that the practice of Catholicism in the United States may differ from the formal position of the Catholic Church.

Because state policy choices are the product of state political processes, the literature examines a series of political explanations for reproductive rights. While some literature (Baker et al., 1981; Medoff, 2002; Medoff et al., 1995) finds that abortion is an issue that often cuts across party lines, Strickland and Whicker (1992) find that political explanations are more important since the *Webster* decision in 1989. Since the *Webster* decision marks the beginning of a trend toward greater state autonomy in abortion policy, it follows that political explanations at the state level – party control of the policy making institutions – are becoming more important (Norrander & Wilcox, 1999). Kahane (1994) reports that the policy position on abortion taken by a governor is significantly influenced by both personal and public (citizen) ideology. While Schecter (2001) suggests that partisanship, gender, and religion of a legislator are all predictors of votes on reproductive rights issues, Kahane (1994), Norrander and Wilcox (1999), and Medoff (2002) all suggest that party control of the legislature is a better predictor of restrictiveness – that Democratic control of state legislatures will result in less restrictive policies.

While party control of state legislatures has tended to change in the past 30 years, perhaps the most concentrated change in party control has been in the South. Once considered a bastion of the Democratic Party, significant changes began to manifest themselves in the late 1980s and 1990s resulting in significant inroads for the Republican Party in both legislative and gubernatorial control (Buchanan, 2009). However, we would not expect this relationship to differ between southern states and the rest of the nation in our observational time frame (2012-2018).

Another important political element concerns the number of females in state legislatures (see Kreitzer, 2015). Norrander and Wilcox (1999) report a positive and significant correlation between the number of women in a legislature and the less restrictive abortion policies, a finding confirmed by Caiazza (2004), Medoff (2002), and Schecter (2001). Caiazza (2004) and Kreitzer (2015) also found that gender tends to temper other factors; female Republican legislators are more likely to vote for less restrictive policies than their male Republican counterparts.

A Religion Explanation

Previous research has explored the importance of religion in predicting attitudes on abortion (see Greentree et al., 2012; Jelen & Wilcox,

2003). Blake and Del Pinal (1981) concluded that abortion was primarily a religious issue, and Jelen and Wilcox (2003) reported that evangelical Protestants were less likely to support abortion rights than those identifying with other religions. Evans (2002) reported that many of the active anti-abortion groups, such as the Christian Coalition and Concerned Women for America, draw significant numbers of their members from evangelical populations. Evans also finds that the Right to Life Committee was created by the Roman Catholic Church to organize local parishes to lobby for anti-abortion legislation. This position is consistent with long-standing opposition of the Catholic Church to abortion dating back to Pope Pius IX's revision of Canon Law (Legge, 1983). Finally, Cook et al. (1993) noted that states with a strong Roman Catholic presence might provide increased support for antichoice policies, but they also report that such a presence may spawn the mobilization of pro-choice movements in those states. Other studies (see Norrander & Wilcox, 1999) failed to detect the same counter-mobilization in states with a strong evangelical population, leading them to suggest that the organizational strength of the Catholic Church was responsible for the difference.

States with a large Jewish population are likely to be less restrictive. Testimony given before the US Senate by the Executive Director of the American Jewish Congress, reprinted in *The New York Times* in 1989, summarized their religious reasoning for their support of abortion rights: "[This religious] tradition believes that the sacredness of life requires in some circumstances that the woman's well-being takes precedence over that of the fetus" ("Open Letter," 1989). This position is bolstered by Greentree et al. (2012), who report that a higher percentage of Jewish citizens in a state tended to reduce that state's level of restrictiveness as measured by the NARAL score.

Given the relatively large evangelical populations found in southern states, we would expect to find more restrictive policies in these states than in non-southern states. Likewise, given the relatively small Catholic populations in most southern states (save Louisiana, Texas, and Florida), we would expect the effects of the percentage of Catholics in southern states to have a negligible effect on restrictiveness. Additionally, the relatively small Jewish populations in southern states (with the possible exception of Florida) would also tend to have little effect on the observed policy restrictiveness, when compared to non-southern states. The model in this chapter thus adds data on the percentages of different religious groups within a state as an additional factor; data for the dependent variable are from NARAL (2012–2018). Table 5.1 presents the descriptive statistics for the variables in our model.

Table 5.1 Descriptive Statistics: Reproductive Rights

	Obsv	Mean	Sd	Min	Max
Dependent variable	350	3.55	1.65	1	5
Republican gubernatorial control	350	.62	.49	0	1
Republican legislative control	343	.59	.49	0	1
Citizen ideology	350	40.92	17.51	17.51	73.49
Poverty	350	10.27	2.84	4	19.20
Minority population	350	20.08	11.43	3	57.70
Unemployment	350	6.96	2.21	2.6	13.1
Catholic	350	19.30	8.66	4	44
Evangelical	350	18.40	9.41	3	43
Jewish	350	1.29	1.13	.5	7
Percent metro	350	202.33	262.20	1	1218
Women in congress	350	24.42	7.06	10	42
South	350	.22	.41	0	1

Analysis

In terms of the dependent variable, there is little variation in the NARAL scores of southern states during the study period. All the observations for southern states are clustered at the "restrictive" end of the scale, with 73 of the 77 state-year observations scored as 5 (the most restrictive score). Indeed, a *t*-test of the dependent variable by South/non-South reveals a mean difference of 1.7905, or nearly 40 percent of the range of the variable. The South is clearly different from the rest of the nation in terms of the magnitude of restrictiveness, but do the same explanations for this restrictiveness hold for the South and the non-South?

The analyses for this policy area produce a particularly robust baseline model (all states; see Table 5.2), with 72 percent of the variance explained. Indeed, the only variables that fail to reach significance in the baseline model are percent Catholic and percent evangelical, although both produce coefficients in the expected direction. This finding echoes Norrander and Wilcox (1999) and Cook et al. (1993), who report that strong Catholic populations can spawn stronger pro-choice movements. Somewhat surprisingly, the coefficient for Republican gubernatorial control is negative, suggesting that states led by Republican governors are less likely to have restrictive policies. We suspect this has more to do with factors other than policy preference; it may speak to the relative influence of a governor in policy choices. Overall, the findings in this model are consistent with previous studies (e.g., Greentree et al., 2012; Jelen & Wilcox, 2003; Schecter, 2001).

When we compare the South to the non-South, we find fewer differences between the groups. For the non-South, Republican gubernatorial control is

Table 5.2 Regression Results: Reproductive Rights

	Baseline Regression	Non-South	South
Republican Gubernatorial Control	−.47**	−.69***	.09
	(.19)	(.25)	(.11)
Republican Legislative Control	.92***	.67***	−.27
	(.20)	(.26)	(.23)
Citizen Ideology	−.04***	−.05***	.01
	(.01)	(.01)	(.01)
Poverty	.12***	.14***	.03
	(.03)	(.04)	(.02)
Minority Population	−.02***	−.02***	.01
	(.01)	(.01)	(.01)
Unemployment	−.14***	−.16***	−.07***
	(.03)	(.04)	(.02)
Catholic	.01	−.01	−.01
	(.01)	(.01)	(.01)
Evangelical	.01	.02*	−.01
	(.01)	(.01)	(.01)
Jewish	−.26***	−.27***	.09
	(.06)	(.07)	(.08)
Percent Metro	.01***	.01***	.01
	(.01)	(.01)	(.01)
Women In Congress	−.03***	−.04***	−.02**
	(.01)	(.01)	(.01)
South	.43**		
	(.17)		
Constant	5.37***	6.29***	5.61***
	(.67)	(.93)	(.58)
Adjusted R2	.72	.69	.17
N =	343	238	77

Note: Standard errors in parentheses. Levels of statistical significance: * 0.1; ** 0.05; *** 0.01. Bold coefficients indicate a significant difference at the 0.1 level in the effects for non-South versus South.

negative and significant, but positive and insignificant for the South. During the study period few southern states had Democratic governors, so there is little variation on which to build. The effect of Republican legislative control is much more apparent in the non-South, but as before, few southern states did not have Republican legislative control during the study period. Several other variables, including citizen ideology, percent minority population, percent evangelical, and percent Jewish produce coefficients with opposite signs between the two models, but in cases in which the variable fails to reach significance in one model or the other. For example, percent Jewish is significant at the $p = .001$ level for the non-South, but the variable is insignificant for the South. The lack of significance is due to the lack of variation across the southern states, which generally have very low numbers of Jewish residents compared to non-South states. The model for the South produces a relatively weak adjusted r^2 of 0.17.

Discussion/Conclusion

The political battle over reproductive rights for women, and particularly over access to abortion services, has been one of the most contentious in American politics in recent memory. Often framed by antichoice advocates as a moral, philosophical, and religious issue, it is not a surprise that the South should be regionally distinct in terms of reproductive rights. In a sense, the South exhibits all the characteristics of opposition to reproductive rights: a strong evangelical population, conservative citizen ideology, single-party (Republican) control, and very small Jewish populations. This is not to say that other states outside the South do not exhibit similar traits; they do. However, the high degree of homogeneity among southern states clearly differentiates the South as region, and highlights the policy differences such homogeneity engenders.

In recent years, southern states have become battlegrounds for the efforts of antichoice groups to press for state legislation to limit access to reproductive services for women. States, such as Louisiana, Alabama, Georgia, and Mississippi, have seen the introduction, and passage, of state legislation aimed at the criminalization of abortion services and their providers. While several of the more draconian measures have been successfully challenged in court, the efforts to overturn *Roe v. Wade* have been especially prevalent in the South. Driven by Republican-controlled legislatures and governor's mansions, coupled with a generally conservative citizenry, southern states have been ready and willing "test cases" for more restrictive legislation. Arkansas recently passed what is considered to be the most restrictive state law to date (Diaz, 2021), and is currently being appealed in federal court.

In their book *The Resilience of Southern Identity*, Cooper and Knotts (2017) do not treat religion as a key component of southern identity, focusing instead on factors such as race, culture, food, and ideology. Other observers, however, such as Elazar (1984), Woodard (2013), and Kellstedt (1990) all point to the influence of religion, and particularly evangelical denominations, in southern politics. To the extent those opposed to reproductive rights for women have been successful in framing the policy issue as a moral and religious issue, it follows that southern states would be more restrictive in their policies than other states. Cooper and Knotts (2017) also report that conservatives are more likely to identify as southerners than are liberals; given the overwhelming conservative ideology present in the South, our findings here come as no surprise.

Appendix

The policies examined and ranked by NARAL for the study years are as follows:

- Abortion bans.
- Biased counseling and mandatory delays.
- Counseling ban/gag rules.
- Access to emergency contraception.
- The Freedom of Choice Act.
- Spousal consent/notice laws.
- Insurance coverage for contraception.
- Insurance prohibition for abortion.
- Legislative declarations.
- Trigger laws.
- Physician-only restrictions.
- Post-viability restrictions.
- Protection against clinic violence legislation.
- Public facilities and public employees' restrictions.
- Refusals to provide medical services (i.e., abortion, contraception, family planning/birth control, sterilization, individual health care instructions, or prescriptions).
- Restrictions on low-income and young women's access to abortions.
- Targeted Regulation of Abortion Providers (TRAP) laws.
- Whether or not the state had codified the protection of the right to choose in its state constitution.

Note

1 An exception to this was *Burwell v. Hobby Lobby Stores* (2014). In this Supreme Court case, the Court ruled that the Affordable Care Act's provision that required employee-sponsored health-care policies to provide contraceptives to employees was unconstitutional. The Court ruled that such a requirement violated the First Amendment rights of the Green family, who owned the corporation, and whose religious views disavowed the use of contraceptives.

References

Aistrup, J.A. (2010). Southern political exceptionalism? Presidential voting in the South and non-South. *Social Science Quarterly, 91*(4), 906–927.

Appelbome, P. (1996). *Dixie rising: How the South is shaping American values, politics, and culture.* Harcourt & Brace.

Baker, R.K., Epstein, L.K., & Forth, R.D. (1981). Matters of life and death: Social, political and religious correlates of attitudes on abortion. *American Politics Quarterly, 9*(January), 89–102.

Barkan, S.E. (2014). Gender and abortion attitudes: religiosity as a suppressor variable. *Public Opinion Quarterly, 78*(4), 940–950.

Blake, J., & Del Pinal, J.H. (1981). Negativism, equivocation and wobbly assent: Public 'support' for the pro-choice platform on abortion. *Demography, 18*(August), 309–320.

Breaux, D.A., Duncan, C.M., Keller, C.D., & Morris, J.C. (2002). Welfare reform, Mississippi style: Temporary Assistance for Needy Families and the search for accountability. *Public Administration Review, 62*(1), 92–103.

Buchanan, S. (2009). The continued convergence of demographics and issues. In B.D. Kapeluck, L. Moreland, & R. Steed (Eds.), *A paler shade of red* (pp. 3–17). University of Arkansas Press.

Burwell v. Hobby Lobby Stores, Inc., 573 US 682 (2014).

Caiazza, A. (2004). Does women's representation in elected office lead to women-friendly policy? Analysis of state-level data. *Women & Politics, 26*(1), 35–70.

Centers for Disease Control and Prevention. (2000). *Abortion surveillance- United States*. US Government Printing Office.

Cook, E.A., Jelen, T.G., & Wilcox, C. (1993). Catholicism and abortion attitudes in the American states: A contextual analysis. *Journal for the Scientific Study of Religion, 32*, 375–383.

Cooper, C., & Knotts, H.G. (2017). *The resilience of southern identity: Why the South still matters in the minds of its people*. University of North Carolina Press.

Diaz, J. (2021). *Arkansas passes near-total abortion ban- and a possible 'Roe v. Wade' test*. NPR. https://www.npr.org/2021/03/10/975546070/arkansas-passes -near-total-abortion-ban-as-lawmakers-push-for-supreme-court-case.

Elazar, D.J. (1984). *American federalism: A view from the states*. Harper & Row.

Evans, J.H. (2002). Polarization in abortion attitudes in U.S. religious traditions, 1972–1998. *Sociological Forum, 17*(3), 397–422.

Gohmann, S.F., & Ohsfeldt, R.L. (1994). Which states will restrict abortions? Predictions from votes in the house of representatives. *Policy Studies Review, 13*, 19–38.

Greentree, V.W., Lombard, J.R., & Morris, J.C. (2012). A comparative analysis of the determinants of state reproductive healthcare policies. *American Review of Politics, 32*, 281–299.

Haas-Wilson, D. (1996). The impact of state abortion restrictions on minors' demand for abortion. *The Journal of Human Resources, 31*(1), 140–158.

Hansen, S. (1980). State implementation of Supreme Court decisions: Abortion rates since Roe v. Wade. *Journal of Politics, 42*(2), 372–395.

Hussey, L.S. (2010). Welfare generosity, abortion access, and abortion rates: A comparison of state policy tools. *Social Science Quarterly, 91*(1), 266–283.

Jelen, T.G., & Wilcox, C. (2003). Causes and consequences of public attitudes toward abortion: A review and research agenda. *Political Research Quarterly, 56*(4), 489–500.

Kahane, L.H. (1994). Political, ideological, and economic determinants of abortion position: An empirical analysis of state legislatures and governors. *American Journal of Economics and Sociology, 53*(3), 347–360.

Key, V.O. (1949). *Southern politics in state and nation.* University of Alabama Press.

Kellstedt, L.A. (1990). Evangelical religion and support for social issue policies: An examination of regional variation. In R. Steed, L.W. Moreland, & T.A. Baker (Eds.), *The disappearing South? Studies in regional change and continuity* (pp. 107–124). University of Alabama Press.

Kreitzer, R.J. (2015). Politics and morality in state abortion policy. *State Politics & Policy Quarterly, 15*(1), 41–66.

Legge, J. (1983). The determinants of attitudes toward abortion in the American electorate. *The Western Political Quarterly, 36*(3), 479–490.

Medoff, M. (2002). The determinants and impact of state abortion restrictions. *American Journal of Economics and Sociology, 61*(2), 481–493.

Medoff, M.H., Dennis, C., & Bishin, B. G. (1995). Bimodal issues, the median voter model, legislator's ideology, and abortion. *Atlantic Economic Journal, 23*(4), 293–303.

National Abortion Rights Action League (NARAL). (2006). *Who decides? The status of women's reproductive rights in the United States* (15th ed.). National Abortion Rights Action League.

National Abortion Rights Action League (NARAL). (2012). *Who decides? The status of women's reproductive rights in the United States* (21st ed.). National Abortion Rights Action League.

National Abortion Rights Action League (NARAL). (2013). *Who decides? The status of women's reproductive rights in the United States* (22nd ed.). National Abortion Rights Action League.

National Abortion Rights Action League (NARAL). (2014). *Who decides? The status of women's reproductive rights in the United States* (23rd ed.). National Abortion Rights Action League.

National Abortion Rights Action League (NARAL). (2015). *Who decides? The status of women's reproductive rights in the United States* (24th ed.). National Abortion Rights Action League.

National Abortion Rights Action League (NARAL). (2016). *Who decides? The status of women's reproductive rights in the United States* (25th ed.). National Abortion Rights Action League.

National Abortion Rights Action League (NARAL). (2017). *Who decides? The status of women's reproductive rights in the United States* (26th ed.). National Abortion Rights Action League.

National Abortion Rights Action League (NARAL). (2018). *Who decides? The status of women's reproductive rights in the United States* (27th ed.). National Abortion Rights Action League.

New, M.J. (2011). Analyzing the effect of anti-abortion US state legislation in the post-Casey era. *State Politics & Policy Quarterly, 11*(1), 28–47.

Norrander, B., & Wilcox, C. (1999). Public opinion and policymaking in the states: The case of post-Roe abortion policy. *Policy Studies Journal, 27*(4), 707–722.

Oakley, M.R. (2003). Abortion restrictions and abortion rates: Has state abortion policy been successful? *Politics and Policy, 31*(3), 1–16.

Open Letter. (1989). Open letter to those who would outlaw abortion. *The New York Times*, Feb. 28.

Planned Parenthood of Southeastern Pennsylvania v. Casey, 505 US 833. (1992).

Roe v. Wade, 410 US 113 (1973).

Schecter, D. (2001). What drives the voting on abortion policy? Investigating partisanship and religion in the state legislative arena. *Women & Politics*, *3*, 61–84.

Soss, J., Schram, S., Vartanian, T., & O'Brien, E. (2001). Setting the terms of relief: Explaining state policy choices in the devolution revolution. *American Journal of Political Science*, *45*(2), 378–395.

Strickland, R.A., & Whicker, M.L. (1992). Political and socioeconomic indicators of state restrictiveness toward abortion. *Policy Studies Journal*, *20*(4), 598–617.

Strickler, J., & Danigelis, N. (2002). Changing frameworks in attitudes toward abortion. *Sociological Forum*, *17*(2), 187–201.

Webster v. Reproductive Health Services, 492 US 490. (1989).

Wetstein, M.E. & Albritton, R.B. (1995). Effects of public opinion on abortion policies and use in the American states. *Publius: The Journal of Federalism*, *25*(4), 91–105.

Woodard, J.D. (2013). *The new southern politics* (2nd ed.). Lynne Reiner Publishers.

6   State Commitment to Clean Water

The issue of water quality has been a prominent component of national environmental policy since the passage of the Federal Water Pollution Control Act (P.L. 80-845) in 1948. Over the years, a series of updates and amendments has sought to strengthen water quality policy; at the same time, the balance between the national government and states has been defined and redefined. While the first three decades of water quality policy identified an increasingly prominent role for the federal government, the last three decades have seen something of a decline in national government authority in this policy arena, and a concomitant growth in state authority and responsibility.

In between these periods of time, the 1972 amendments to the Federal Water Pollution Control Act, more commonly known as the Clean Water Act (CWA), were enacted. Although the CWA was in some ways an incremental shift from previous water quality legislation, it contained several important elements. First, the CWA contained a much-expanded role for the national government in terms of water quality legislation, and it established a national water quality goal. The CWA also greatly expanded the existing categorical grant mechanism, the construction grants program, to help municipalities fund water quality infrastructure (treatment plants, sewer collection systems, etc.). However, the construction grants program was administered by the federal government, which meant that states were largely removed from the funding decisions for water quality in their respective states.

The landscape of water quality policy was changed significantly with the passage of the Water Quality Act (WQA) (P.L. 100-4) in 1987. While the WQA contained a number of changes to the CWA, one of the most important changes was a switch from a categorical grant to a block grant program as embodied in Title VI of the WQA. Under Title VI, states would receive capitalization grants from the national government and would match those grants with a state-funded 20 percent contribution. The funds would then

DOI: 10.4324/9781003134602-6

be placed in a state-administered fund from which states would make loans to communities within the state to meet water quality needs in the state. The loans would be paid back by communities, and the loan repayments (principal and interest) would then be repurposed in the form of new loans to other communities. Known as the Clean Water State Revolving Fund (CWSRF) program, the program design was intended to return responsibility for wastewater needs to the states (see Morris, 1997). Although the CWSRF program was only authorized through the Fiscal Year 1994 (and, to date, has not been reauthorized), Congress has continued to appropriate grant funds for the CWSRF program every year since the passage of the legislation.

The CWSRF program is one of the longest lived examples of Reagan federalism (see Morris, 1999). An advocate for states' rights, President Ronald Reagan championed a reduction in the size, scope, and cost of the national government, and a return of greater authority and fiscal responsibility to the states. This was a message that particularly resonated in southern states, in that the issue of states' rights (in various guises) had been a grievance (and interest) of southern states since the American Revolution. In this sense, we would expect that southern states would embrace the CWSRF model since it would provide states with enhanced decision-making power, a ready source of funds, and empower the states to determine how those funds were to be allocated. Conversely, the WQA and its predecessor, the CWA, are also regulatory in nature, and southern states are not known to be in the vanguard of environmental protection, inasmuch as environmental regulation is often viewed by southern states as an example of unnecessary government regulation (see Emison & Morris, 2010). With these potentially conflicting incentives in mind, the question for this chapter is as follows: do southern states exhibit different patterns of resource distribution in the CWSRF program than do non-southern states?

The Mechanism of the Revolving Loan Fund Model

The use of a revolving loan fund model to meet wastewater infrastructure needs was proposed in a report prepared by a working group within the US Environmental Protection Agency (EPA) in 1984. Realizing that the construction grants program was becoming politically unpopular, the working group was charged with the development of future options for wastewater funding. The group realized that the net effect of the construction grants program since 1972 had been the steady reduction of state and local funding efforts so that the national government was now bearing the brunt of the cost of clean water (EPA, 1984). Their report offered several alternatives to restructure water quality finance. However, the commentary made clear that the working group's preference was for a revolving loan model. The model was incorporated into the WQA almost exactly as proposed.

The logic behind the revolving loan model is that states would use the federal capitalization grant, along with the required 20 percent match, to create a state-administered loan from which construction loans would be made to communities in the state. The state would have authority over the requirements for eligibility, the interest rate structure and duration of the loans, and the decisions over recipient communities. In this manner, the states would assume responsibility for all aspects of the program. The WQA did place some requirements and limitations on states regarding loan amortization, a requirement for the fund to remain financially solvent in perpetuity, and the kinds of communities Congress wished to be served under the program: communities with significant environmental need, small communities (defined as communities with populations under 3,500), and financially at-risk communities. In addition, the WQA allowed states to use CWSRF funds to capitalize projects intended to address nonpoint pollution,[1] a category of pollution heretofore not generally addressed by the construction grants program. Outside of these limitations, states were free to structure the program as they saw fit.

The EPA realized very early that the funds authorized under the WQA were inadequate to capitalize the state programs to the point where states would truly be self-sufficient. To this end, the EPA encouraged states to engage in leveraging, which would use the capitalization grants as a reserve for state-supported bond issues. The contemplated bond issues would raise additional funds but would also increase the cost of borrowing for applicant communities (see Holcombe, 1992). States thus had to decide whether leveraging was worthwhile. As noted earlier in this chapter, while the original authorization of $9.6 billion in the WQA expired in FY 1994, Congress has actually appropriated CWSRF capitalization grants every year since. Even with the additional capitalization grants, only about half of all states have leveraged their capitalization grants in at least one year.

A Model of State Choice in the CWSRF Program

The question in this chapter addresses the ways in which states allocate their CWSRF funds, particularly in terms of the intent of Congress as stated in the WQA. To this end, we focus our attention on the annual amount of money loaned to meet significant environmental needs. These needs are the focus of the CWSRF program, as evidenced by the "first use" requirement that obligates states to use all CWSRF funds initially to meet environmental needs. This requirement, captured in Title VI of the WQA, ensures that the CWSRF program remains focused as an environmental program. We examine whether the distribution patterns in southern states are different than the distribution patterns found in states outside the South.

Previous Studies of the CWSRF Program

Scholarly work published in the early years of the CWSRF program (see Heilman & Johnson, 1991; Holcombe, 1992; Morris, 1994, 1997, 1999) set the groundwork for much of the later work in the field. Heilman and Johnson (1991) first described the wide variation in state approaches to CWSRF implementation and cataloged some of the differences in state implementation. They also noted the pressure by the EPA on states to engage in leveraging and explored the reasons why states made leveraging choices. Holcombe (1992) built an economic model of the long-term effects of leveraging, along with an analysis of the effects of different interest rates and inflation rates on long-term CWSRF fund viability. He noted that the interest rate charged on loans must be higher than the prevailing rate of inflation for the fund to remain viable; the need to pay interest on leveraged bonds pushes interest rates even higher.

Morris (1994, 1997, 1999) examined several specific elements of CWSRF program implementation, including the differences in loan distribution patterns among the states when private sector actors are incorporated into CWSRF funding decisions. His findings indicated that states with higher levels of private sector involvement in CWSRF administration were less likely to make loans to small communities or financially at-risk communities. Other significant elements of state choice in the CWSRF program included political culture, state administrative capacity, and the administrative location of the CWSRF program in state government.

Travis et al. (2004) conducted an in-depth examination of state leveraging decisions. They found that the reasons for leveraging promulgated by the EPA – environmental need and a demand for loans from communities – failed to predict state funding decisions. They also determined that leveraging was best conceived as a two-stage decision: a decision whether to leverage, and then a second decision to determine how *much* to leverage. Bunch (2008) reported a relationship between interest rates charged on loans and the value of the packages of state and federal assistance offered to applicant communities. Mullin and Daley (2018) noted a positive link between CWSRF funds and state and local spending on water infrastructure, and Arbuckle (2013) noted that CWSRF recipients were more likely to invest in conservation projects. Morris et al. (2021) and Williamson et al. (2021) found that political culture, institutional location, state centralization, professionalization, population, and a unified Democratic legislature were reliably predictive variables to explain loan distribution patterns. To date, there is no work that explicitly addresses differences in water quality between southern states and the rest of the nation.

Measures of Need in the CWSRF Program

Unlike other policy arenas, measuring need in the CWSRF program is challenging in that there are no widely employed and widely accepted measures of water quality improvement. However, states are required under the law to carry out an assessment of the dollar value of water quality infrastructure needs in the state and report this information to the EPA (see EPA, 2016). In lieu of a comparable measure common to states to measure the condition of waterways in the state, we employ this measure of infrastructure needs. The needs survey captures specific needs in seven different categories; the two most critical categories are Category I (secondary waste treatment) and Category II (advanced wastewater treatment). A treatment plant that does not meet Category I and II needs is an indication of significant environmental needs as defined in the WQA (EPA, 2016). Although the values in the report are self-reported by states, they are the best existing indication of relative state need for water quality resources. Furthermore, while it is likely that there is a degree of overestimation in the reported values, it is reasonable to assume that the states are overestimating their needs in comparable ways, and that the error in these estimates is randomly distributed across all states. We also note that the needs assessment does not require states to report needs for different classes of communities (e.g., small communities or financially at-risk communities) or for nonpoint pollution needs, so the data only represent total need in the state. With limited funds available, states must make choices about how to allocate CWSRF resources across all of these needs and types of applicants. If a state has significant needs for Category I and Category II projects, for instance, it is reasonable to suggest that states will direct resources for these needs rather than, for example, nonpoint source needs.

Hypotheses

Our dependent variable in this study is the standardized value of loans made for Category I and Category II needs by each state in each year during our study period. The data are drawn from EPA (2020a), as are data for annual state contributions. Data for both state contribution and the dependent variable are adjusted for inflation, and the variable is transformed to allow for easier interpretation of the coefficients.

In addition to the relationships developed earlier in the volume for the general model of state policymaking, we offer the following hypotheses regarding state needs for water quality. First, states with greater documented needs for Category I and Category II projects are more likely to make loans to applicants with significant environmental needs. States are also able to decide the institutional location of the CWSRF program. Previous studies (see Morris, 2022) suggest that the three most common agencies are state environmental agencies, health agencies, and finance agencies. A small handful of states locate the program in a different agency; these are coded for our purposes as "other." Because environmental agencies exist to implement environmental programs, we hypothesize that programs located in environmental agencies are more likely to focus on environmental needs than programs located elsewhere.

Under the Water Quality Act, states are required to provide 20 percent of the value of the federal grant in matching funds. In addition, states are encouraged to allocate additional dollars to their CWSRF funds in the form of additional appropriations or, more commonly through the use of leveraging techniques as a means to increase the size of the pool of dollars available. If states contribute additional funds to the program, more dollars will be available to make loans.

As a measure of state commitment to water quality, we employ the year in which the state first achieved primacy in water quality. A feature of the Clean Water Act, primacy is awarded to states that agree to assume responsibility for regulatory enforcement for water pollution in their state. Awarded by the EPA, primacy is an agreement on the part of states to ensure that state and federal clean water standards are met. The first year primacy was available was 1973; as of 2019, all but four states had assumed primacy; the most recent state to achieve primacy did so in 2016.

The Clean Water Act required states to report the dollar value of their water quality infrastructure needs to EPA every four years. Referred to as the Clean Water Needs Survey, the document contains estimates of the current needs of states in terms of dollars needed to meet water quality standards. This measure is widely employed in water quality studies as a state-level environmental need measure; however, the most recent report publicly available is for 2012, published in 2016 (EPA, 2016). For this study, we use a measure of the combined needs for Category I needs (secondary treatment) and Category II needs (advanced) treatment. Under the WQA, these two categories of need are defined as "significant environmental need."

Finally, in terms of the variables from our basic model, we expect to see Republican governors direct fewer resources to environmental needs. As poverty and percent minority increase, we would expect to see fewer resources directed to significant environmental needs. In terms of differences between the South and the non-South, we expect differences in terms of institutional location, since most southern states locate their programs in environmental agencies. Table 6.1 displays the summary statistics for the variables in our model.

Analysis

Based on the model developed in the preceding section, we now turn to our analyses. Table 6.2 presents the results of the model. As with previous chapters, we present three models: a baseline (50-state) model, a non-South model, and a South model. For our baseline model, both poverty and percent minority, two variables from our base model, are positive and significant. Republican gubernatorial control fails to reach significance, but this finding is not unexpected. The CWSRF program is largely implemented by state agencies, and governors (and legislatures) generally do not play a role in state funding decisions. Both may be involved in decisions regarding state contributions, but these are rarely partisan issues. The one instance in which partisan politics might be involved is the case in which a state appropriates additional state funds to the program but that has only happened in the years prior to our study period. On the other hand, we find strong support for two of our hypotheses specific to water quality. The "primacy year" variable is strongly significant; states who have exercised primacy for a longer period of time are more likely to direct CWSRF funds to communities with significant environmental needs. Likewise, our need measure is also strongly positive and significant, suggesting that states apply their CWSRF funds as a means to reduce the backlog of infrastructure needs. Finally, the dummy variable for "South" is also significant and negative, suggesting that southern states are significantly different from non-South states.

Table 6.1 Descriptive Statistics: Water Quality

	Obsv	Mean	SD	Min	Max
Dependent variable	350	.01	1.01	−.58	8.81
Republican gubernatorial control	350	.62	.49	0	1
Poverty	350	10.27	2.84	4	19.2
Minority	350	20.08	11.43	3	57.7
State contributions	350	2.04e-08	1	−.73	5.44
Institutional location					
Environmental	347	.70	.46	0	1
Health	347	.08	.08	0	1
Financial	347	.18	.18	0	1
Other	347	.04	.04	0	1
Primacy year	329	1,980.92	10.84	1,973	2,019
Added needs	350	2,043.07	2,818.47	0	13,953.39
South	350	.22	.41	0	1

Table 6.2 Regression Results: Water Quality

	Baseline Regression	Non-South	South
Republican gubernatorial control	−.10	−.11	−.08
	(.07)	(.09)	(.26)
Poverty	.04**	.01	.01
	(.02)	(.02)	(.04)
Minority	.01*	−.01	−.02
	(.01)	(.01)	(.01)
State contributions	.10	.07	.15
	(.09)	(.01)	(.14)
Institutional location			
Health	−.07	−.11	.19
	(.11)	(.11)	(.29)
Financial	−.12	**−.28****	**.35**
	(.12)	(.13)	(.37)
Other	.13	−.06	1.26**
	(.13)	(.12)	(.62)
Primacy year	−.01***	−.01**	−.02**
	(.01)	(.01)	(.01)
Added needs	.01***	.01***	.01***
	(.01)	(.01)	(.01)
South	−.50***		
	(.15)		
Constant	23.84***	9.00**	47.06**
	(6.10)	(4.46)	(23.05)
R^2	.47	.53	.45
N=	326	221	77

Note: Standard errors in parentheses. Levels of statistical significance: * 0.1; ** 0.05; *** 0.01. Bold coefficients indicate a significant difference at the 0.1 level in the effects for non-South versus South.

The non-South model produces a somewhat different picture. None of the variables in the basic model reach statistical significance, although all the coefficients are in the expected direction. One difference is in the institutional location variable; for the non-South, programs located in financial agencies are less likely to direct CWSRF funds to communities with significant environmental needs. This finding is counter to Morris (2022), who reports that financial agencies are generally employed in states that leverage their CWSRF funds. Because leveraging increases the amount of money available for loans, states are better able to direct resources to meet environmental needs. Morris' (2022) study covers the period from 1988 to 2016; it may be the case that patterns of activity in the early years of the program are different than more recent patterns. As is the case with the baseline model, primacy year and added needs remain strong predictors of the dependent variable.

The South model follows a pattern similar to the non-South. One surprising difference is again found in the institutional location variable. In this model, all three alternative locations – health agencies, financial agencies, and other agencies – direct a greater share of CWSRF resources to significant environmental needs than do environmental agencies. Although only the "other" category is the only one to reach statistical significance, the positive coefficients suggest an interesting dynamic in CWSRF administration in southern states. The other CWSRF-specific variables in the model – primacy year and added needs – perform as expected and are significant. In all three of the models, the explained variance is reasonably strong, accounting for roughly half of the variance in each case.

Discussion/Conclusion

The case of water quality illustrates a policy arena in which the differences between the South and the non-South are relatively minor. At one level, water quality seems to be a reasonably benign policy space: people everywhere care about water quality, and there is no compelling reason to think that Southerners are any different in this regard. However, previous work (see Emison & Morris, 2010) indicates that southern states are distinct from the rest of the nation in terms of environmental policy. These differences are not driven by attitudes toward the environment, but rather by ideas about the proper role of government coupled with factors such as wealth, taxation, and commitment to environmental protection. In the case of the latter factor, resistance to government regulation tends to drive the level of commitment. Interestingly, all southern states have accepted primacy, and about half of the states accepted primacy within the first 15 years of availability. While this may be interpreted as a commitment to the environment, in the case of southern states it may also be driven by a very different motivation: states' rights. Southern states were generally early implementers of the CWSRF program (see Morris, 2022); moreover, the underlying logic of the CWSRF program was a reflection of Reagan federalism, which was based on a state-centric model of federalism (Morris, 1999). This approach had great appeal for southern states.

Historically, southern states were largely rural and agrarian, which made the use of centralized wastewater treatment infrastructure impractical. As the populations of southern states grew and towns and cities grew, the need for centralized treatment became more acute. Southern states are also generally less affluent and have a lower tax effort, which translates into fewer dollars available to meet environmental imperatives. A *t*-test of the mean

CWSRF dollars spent for significant environmental needs suggests a difference significant at the 0.1 level, further suggesting the differences between the South and non-South is relatively small.

Taken as a whole, the arena of water quality does not suggest a remarkable difference in policy outcomes in the South. Although southern states achieve water quality outcomes in different ways than non-southern states, the net result is not very much different. Unexplored in our model, but that might become part of a larger study focusing on broad environmental commitment, is the role of overall state commitment to water policy. Such a study might examine not only a focus on significant environmental needs but also on the other allowable uses for CWSRF funds, such as loans to small communities, loans to communities facing financial hardship, or loans for nonpoint pollution remediation. Given the general reluctance of southern states to adopt stringent environmental standards (see Emison & Morris, 2010), it may be the case that greater differences would be detected in a broader definition of water infrastructure uses. However, it appears that, in our more limited model, the South is not very different from the rest of the nation.

Note

1 Nonpoint pollution refers to pollution emanating from many diffuse sources, such as runoff from agricultural land, suburban homes, or streets and highways. The Clean Water Act regulates point source pollution, but Congress has explicitly chosen not to regulate nonpoint pollution.

References

Arbuckle, J., Jr. (2013). Clean Water State Revolving Fund loans and landowner investments in agricultural best management practices in Iowa. *Journal of the American Water Resources Association, 49*(1), 67–75.

Bunch, B. (2008). Clean Water State Revolving Fund program: Analysis of variations in state practices. *International Journal of Public Administration, 31*, 117–136.

Emison, G., & Morris, J. (2010). *Speaking green with a southern accent: Environmental management and innovation in the South.* Lexington Books.

Heilman, J., & Johnson, G. (1991). *State revolving loan funds: Analysis of institutional arrangements and distributive consequences.* Auburn University, AL. Final Report Submitted to the U.S. Geological Survey, Department of the Interior.

Holcombe, R. (1992). Revolving fund finance: The case of wastewater treatment. *Public Budgeting & Finance, 12*, 50–65.

Morris, J. (2022; forthcoming). *Clean water policy at state choice: Promise and performance in the Water Quality Act.* Cambridge University Press.

Morris, J. (1999). Was Reagan federalism good for business? Privatization and state administrative capacity in the clean water state revolving fund program. *Southeastern Political Review, 27*(2), 323–339.

Morris, J. (1997). The distributional impacts of privatization in national water quality policy. *Journal of Politics, 59*(1), 56–72.

Morris, J. (1994). *Privatization and environmental policy: An examination of the distributive consequences of private sector activity in State Revolving Funds* (unpublished doctoral dissertation). Auburn University.

Morris, J., Williamson, R., Nguyen, L., & Hume, J. (2021). Promise and performance: The Water Quality Act at thirty. Paper presented at the Annual Meetings of the Southern Political Science Association, January 2021.

Mullin, M., & Daley, D. (2018). Multilevel instruments for infrastructure investment: Evaluating State Revolving Funds for water. *Policy Studies Journal, 46*(3), 629–650.

Travis, R., Morris, E., & Morris, J. (2004). State implementation of federal environmental policy: Explaining leveraging in the Clean Water State Revolving Fund. *Policy Studies Journal, 32*(3), 461–480.

U.S. Environmental Protection Agency (EPA). (2020a). Clean Water State Revolving Fund (CWSRF) national information management system reports. https://www.epa.gov/cwsrf/clean-water-state-revolving-fund-cwsrf-national-information-management-system-reports.

U.S. Environmental Protection Agency (EPA). (2016). *Clean watersheds needs survey 2012: Report to Congress*. USEPA. EPA-830-R-15005.

U.S. Environmental Protection Agency (EPA). (1984). *Study of the future federal role in municipal wastewater treatment: Report to the administrator*. USEPA.

Williamson, R., Morris, J., & Fisk, J. (2021). Institutional variation, professionalization, and state implementation choices: An examination of investment on water quality across the 50 states. *American Review of Public Administration*, 51(6), 436–448.

7   State Firearm Legislation

A storm of recent mass shootings has brought the issue of firearm violence into the policy spotlight. Although these shootings act as focusing events for firearm legislation, they account for less than 0.1 percent of the total firearm-related deaths (Siegel & Boine, 2019). With increased focus on firearm violence comes greater interest in how state and federal governments are responding. There is a substantial literature examining the impact state policies have on firearm violence (see: Kaufman et al., 2018; Kivisto et al., 2017; Rosengart et al., 2005; Ruddel & Mays, 2005); however, little research has examined the explanators of the variation among state firearm policies. Our interest is less in exploring the efficacy of firearm policies than in explaining the conditions in place at the state level that explain the legislation (or lack thereof). This chapter examines a variety of explanations offered for the varying state response to firearm legislation, and whether the responses of southern states differ from those of non-South states.

The dependent variable employed for this research is an index of several categories of state law related to restricting firearm ownership and use. There is wide variation across states in terms of a state's willingness (or ability) to enact firearm legislation. One of the most contentious policy arenas in American politics, the political stakes are equally high on both sides of the debate. This may be especially true in the South. Southerners often combine a healthy contempt for government with a love of the outdoors, hunting, and recreational firearm use, and a strong cultural connection to a "frontier" mentality. But to what degree is the South distinct in this regard, and how does distinctiveness translate into policy choices by southern states?

While much has been written about the effects of various firearm control legislation, we know little about why some states enact firearm control legislation and other states do not. To begin to fill this gap, we employ firearm legislation and demographic data to better understand the conditions in

DOI: 10.4324/9781003134602-7

states that choose to adopt (or to not adopt) firearm legislation and if and how this may differ in the South.

Background

Perhaps one of the most controversial policy issues in American politics today is "gun control." Who can possess firearms, what type of firearms can they possess, and when and where firearms can be displayed or carried, are questions with which politicians constantly struggle. There are conflicting and competing constitutional claims, public opinions, and dogmatic positions concerning the relationship between firearms and safety, and legislators must strike a reasonable balance between these forces when crafting firearm-related legislation.

There is an array of state firearm legislation regulating who can possess firearms and what types of firearms can be possessed. Siegel and Boine (2019) have provided arguably the broadest study of firearm legislation to date. These authors developed a comprehensive database of state firearm legislation for the years 1991–2016. They went on to evaluate the legislation in terms of the impact on firearm-related homicides. The authors argue legislation that addresses who can possess firearms had a greater impact than legislation that addresses what type of firearms can be possessed. Three legislative approaches were identified that greatly impacted firearm-related homicide: (1) universal background checks; (2) "may issue" laws; and (3) laws prohibiting firearm possession by those convicted of violent misdemeanors. Universal background checks are defined as follows: any firearm transaction either through private parties or through a licensed dealer must be preceded by a background check to certify the prospective buyer has not been deemed ineligible to possess a firearm. Siegel and Boine (2019) report states with universal background checks have 9.6 percent fewer firearm-related homicides compared to states without. Legislation that gives law enforcement authorities discretion when approving concealed carry permits is referred to "may issue" laws. Those states with "may issue" laws have 11.1 percent fewer firearm-related homicides than states that do not have that law. One of the greatest predictors of future violence is past violence. States that have included violent misdemeanors as a disqualifier for firearm possession have a 19.3 percent reduction in firearm homicides. However, the most meaningful finding is that states with all three of the laws in place experienced 34.6 percent less firearm homicides over the 25-year period studied (Siegel & Boine, 2019).

Ruddell and Mays (2005) examined whether states with universal background checks had a reduction in firearm-related homicides using the mean number of firearm homicides between 1999 and 2001. The authors controlled for the number of firearms in circulation, violent crime, citizens under community-based supervision, and demographic and economic variables. After adjusting their models several times due to collinearity, the authors conclude that "states that had comprehensive background checks had a consistent negative relationship with state firearms homicide rates" (Ruddell & Mays, 2005, p. 134).

Understanding that offenders often transport firearms from states with less restrictive firearm regulations to states with more restrictive regulations, Kaufman et al. (2018) developed several models to examine whether bordering states were impacted by differing levels of restrictiveness of their neighboring states. They used county-level firearm and suicide rates, both firearm-related and non-firearm-related, as the main outcome measures. Additionally, the authors developed a six-dimension index of firearm restrictiveness to use as an independent variable. This index included universal background checks, a ban on inexpensive "Saturday night special" firearms, multiple gun purchases at one time, laws requiring firearms to be licensed, laws requiring licensing to own a firearm, and laws requiring lost or stolen firearms to be reported. The models also included standard demographic and crime-related variables. The analysis suggested that counties in states with more restrictive firearm policies had lower rates of firearm suicides, irrespective of the strength of neighboring state firearm laws. In addition, the counties in states with more restrictive firearm policies had lower rates of firearm homicides.

Using the 2015 state restrictiveness firearm policy score from the Brady Campaign as their key independent variable, Kivisto et al. (2015) sought to evaluate the impact of firearm policy restrictiveness on rates of fatal police shootings. The index of state firearm policies included seven categories of gun laws based on the laws intended purpose: background checks, restricting firearms in public places, laws that addressed child and consumer safety, laws to curb gun trafficking, restrictions on dangerous weapons, restrictions on dangerous people, and laws that involve a duty to retreat. The model included standard demographic covariates found in the existing literature. The authors argued that more restrictive state firearm laws resulted in lower numbers of fatal police shootings. They concluded that states with the strictest firearm policies experienced as many as 50 percent fewer fatal police shootings than states with the weakest laws.[1]

In an effort to examine whether the strength of state gun laws or the rate of gun ownership had an impact on the number of mass shootings at the state level, Reeping et al. (2019) use a cross-sectional time series model to measure the relationships. The outcome variable number of mass shootings in this study was defined as an event in which four or more people were killed with a firearm. The main independent variable is state level per capita gun ownership. The second independent variable used is an index of restrictiveness/permissiveness for firearm laws in all 50 states as reported in the *Traveler's Guide to the Firearms Laws of the Fifty States*. Additional covariates represent standard demographics, as modeled in previous research. The findings produced by this model suggest that states with more permissive gun laws and higher rates of gun ownership experienced higher rates of mass shootings.

Analyzing the impact of firearm restrictiveness on nonfatal firearm injuries, Simonetti et al. (2015) use cross-sectional discharge records for patients hospitalized for gunshot injuries in the 18 states that report that data for 2010. The data represent individuals treated for gunshot injuries in an inpatient or emergency department and who were discharged alive from that facility. The primary independent variable is the Brady Campaign score of restrictiveness of state firearm policy; covariates include standard demographic variables as reported in previous research. The authors argue that the stricter state-level firearm policy, as represented in the Brady Campaign Index, the lower the number of patients discharged from facilities for nonfatal firearm injuries.

There is one study that uses the Brady Campaign Index of state firearm policy restrictiveness as the outcome measure. Kaskawal (2016) chose three states that scored as "strict," three states that scored as "moderate," and three states that scored as "mildly restrictive" on the Brady Campaign Index. The primary independent variables are nonfatal and fatal firearm rates. Covariates in this study included standard demographic and political variables found in similar literature. The study is inconclusive most likely due to its low sample size and lack of advanced statistical design.

Modeling Firearm Restrictiveness

Our dependent variable consists of an additive index created from data provided by The Rockefeller Institute of Government Regional Gun Violence Consortium's policy brief "What Are the Most Effective Policies in Reducing Gun Homicides?" (Siegel & Boine, 2019). This database lists eight different state laws related to firearm policy, including the year each was enacted. From those eight we used the three laws that showed significant reduction in homicides along with two others that showed promising results. From this, we construct an index that indicates a state's commitment to firearm protection. The specific categories of legislation include the following: buyer regulations (restrictions on bulk firearm purchases); prohibitions for high-risk gun possession (violent offenders); universal background checks; concealed carry permitting ("may issue" laws); and "stand your ground" laws. Because little research of this nature has been conducted, we looked to the general firearm violence and state comparative literature in building the index.

Hypotheses

This chapter analysis focuses squarely on the base model and how it impacts restrictiveness as determined through our construction of the index dependent variable. Within the base model we expect states with Republican leadership (executive and legislature) to be less likely to enact stringent gun regulations. A cornerstone of Republican party dogma is a staunch defense of Second Amendment rights. Bolstered by strong support from pro-gun rights groups such as the National Rifle Association, state-controlled legislatures have been reticent to enact stricter firearm laws. Conversely, we expect states with a more liberal citizenry to enact stricter firearm legislation.

As poverty and minority population increase, we expect to see less strict firearm regulations. Some of this can be explained by the state lens through which we examine the issue, but also by the South, where there are large minority populations, some of the more impoverished states in the country, and generally strong, pro-gun, conservative leadership. Much like the other sociodemographic variable, unemployment rates have been included in various models, including fatal police shooting (Kivisto et al., 2017), firearm homicides (Kaufman et al., 2018), nonfatal firearm injuries (Simonetti et al., 2015), and mass shootings (Reeping et al., 2019) but the results have been mixed. We expect states with higher unemployment to enact stricter firearm legislation.

Analysis

This chapter explores state differences in firearm legislation determined by state action across several equally scored policy windows, including prohibitions for high-risk gun possession (violent offenders), universal background checks, "stand your ground" laws, concealed carry permitting ("may issue" laws), and buyer regulations (restrictions on bulk firearm purchases). Employing common predictors of the state decision-making literature including Republican governorship, Republican-controlled legislature, citizen ideology, percentage minority citizens, poverty rate, and the unemployment rate, this chapter identifies and explains the factors influencing state decision-making toward gun policy restrictiveness. Table 7.1 presents the summary statistics for the variables employed in this analysis.

While the dependent variable components are dichotomous and the index dependent variable can be viewed as categorical, we employ OLS regression because we are treating the five components of support and

Table 7.1 Descriptive Statistics: Firearm Legislation

	Obsv	Mean	SD	Min	Max
Dependent variable	700	1.08	1.19	0	5
Republican gubernatorial control	700	.56	.50	0	1
Republican legislative control	686	.47	.50	0	1
Citizen ideology	650	44.91	16.61	17.51	73.62
Poverty	650	9.97	2.80	4	19.20
Minority population	250	21.12	12.72	1.39	75.05
Unemployment	650	7.08	2.25	2.6	15.1
South	700	.22	.41	0	1

opposition as equivalent in their impact. Table 7.2 presents the results of the OLS regression and the three examined models, the 50-state baseline, the non-South, and South.

Examining the models in the order they appear in the table, the 50-state baseline model, with more than 240 observations over several years has the greatest number of significant predictors of restrictiveness of the three models, while explaining nearly half of the variance within the dependent variable index. For the most part, the variables are in the expected direction: the more liberal citizenry, the more restrictive gun policy; the greater poverty, the less restrictive gun policy; and the greater the minority population the more restrictive. However, the one major surprise in the baseline model is the direction and significance of Republican gubernatorial control. Republican gubernatorial leadership has a statistically significant positive relationship, within this model for predicting gun policy restrictiveness. On the surface, this seems counter-intuitive and there is some correlation concern with the citizen ideology variable. However, after running multiple iterations of the model, transforming variables, and omitting others, the results remain mostly the same. This finding highlights a positive Republican gubernatorial relationship in predicting gun policy restrictiveness within the model. Some of this may be explained by the time frame being analyzed in which Republicans held a substantial advantage in the number of offices held, but it may also suggest simply that citizen ideology ultimately seems to trump traditional partisan executive control.

In examining the non-South, the results mostly mirror the 50-state baseline model in direction and significance with the exception of the minority population variable no longer achieving statistical significance. This suggests to us that Aistrup's (2010) assertion that politics in the South is all about race is accurate. The model itself is slightly weaker, explaining just over 40 percent of the variance.

Moving on to the South as a distinct region, model three is particularly interesting for both what is significant and what is not. In the South model,

Table 7.2 Regression Results: Firearm Legislation

	Baseline Regression	Non-South	South
Republican gubernatorial control	1.22***	1.45***	.48
	(.16)	(.19)	(.25)
Republican legislative control	.20	.25	−.03
	(.18)	(.22)	(.53)
Citizen ideology	.06***	.07***	.04***
	(.01)	(.01)	(.01)
Poverty	−.14***	−.09***	−.16***
	(.02)	(.03)	(.03)
Minority population	.01**	.01	−.01
	(.01)	(.01)	(.01)
Unemployment	.03	.02	.01
	(.03)	(.04)	(.04)
South	−.48		
	(.15)		
Constant	−1.50**	−2.23***	.61
	(.58)	(.70)	(.81)
Adjusted r^2	.46	.41	.55
N =	245	190	55

Note: Standard errors in parentheses. Levels of statistical significance: * 0.1; ** 0.05; *** 0.01.
Bold coefficients indicate a significant difference at the 0.1 level in the effects for non-South versus South.

Republican gubernatorial control is no longer significant. This is particularly interesting because it is the first model that the variable comes back as a non-significant predictor. Further, Republican gubernatorial control is frequently found to be a significant predictor in the state decision-making literature. This result, along with the other models, suggests that something different may be at work here; it may, in part, be due to Republican dominance in southern states during the study period. Like model two, minority population is no longer a significant predictor of restrictiveness, but poverty and citizen ideology are significant. The South model is the strongest of the three, in that it explains 55 percent of the variance within the dependent variable.

The findings are particularly interesting in that we can begin to identify general and regional trends in state decision-making toward gun policy leg-islation. For the most part the models are within striking distance of each other as far as explained variance and significant predictors; however, the South model is the strongest. There is also some evidence for southern distinctiveness, not necessarily for what predicts restrictiveness as much as for what does not. The South model is the only model of the three in which Republican gubernatorial control is found not to be a significant pre-dictor of gun policy restrictiveness. In addition to this kernel of southern distinctiveness, the findings as a whole highlight the importance of ideology and poverty in explaining what drives states in their decisions on gun policy restrictiveness. No matter the model, more liberal states are significantly more likely to implement more restrictive gun policy; conversely, more impoverished states are significantly less restrictive when it comes to gun control policy.

Discussion/Conclusion

Our findings lend evidence that the South continues to retain a regional identity that manifests itself in terms of differences in state policy choices between the South and the rest of the nation. When Steed et al. (1990) asked whether southern distinctiveness was a relic of the past, the evidence was mixed. Indeed, Breaux et al. (2002) suggested that the South was becoming less distinct, but largely because the rest of the nation was becoming more like the South, rather than the inverse. Our findings lend support to the southern distinctiveness hypothesis.

In addition, this research treats firearm policy differently than most of the extant literature. Rather than treating restrictiveness or leniency as an explanator of violence in states, we seek to understand why states make the policy choices they do. In the present case, citizen ideology and minority population appear to drive policy choices. Our findings regarding the impact of Republican-controlled governorships, however, begs for additional thought and research. Given the conventional wisdom in the literature that gun rights and Second Amendment freedoms are core Republican issues, our results require additional effort to more fully understand.

While our research sheds light on state policy choices in the South and the rest of the nation, there is opportunity for further research and refinement. Although it appears that citizen ideology is a critical component of this policy arena, perhaps an analysis that substitutes citizen ideology for a variable such as political culture might yield interesting results. It may be the case, for instance, that traditionalistic and individualistic cultures treat firearm policy much the same, but differently from moralistic cultures. Likewise, our analysis does not consider the effects of party competition on firearm policy; it may be that substituting Republican control for party competitiveness might strengthen our explained variance. These (and other) issues are the subject of ongoing and future research.

Note

1   This study was published with a large caveat, in that there is no official reporting of fatal police shootings, the outcome measure, requiring them to use "crowd-sourced" data sourced by a media outlet.

References

Aistrup, J. (2010). Southern political exceptionalism? Presidential voting in the South and Non-South. *Social Science Quarterly, 91*(4), 906–927.

Breaux, D., Duncan, C., Keller, C., & Morris, J. (2002). Welfare reform, Mississippi style: Temporary Assistance for Needy Families and the search for accountability. *Public Administration Review, 62*(1), 92–103.

Kaskawal, B. (2016). *Determinants of state firearm policy variation* [unpublished honors thesis]. Portland State University.

Kaufman, E., Morrison, C., Branas, C., & Wiebe, D. (2018). State firearm laws and interstate firearm deaths from homicide and suicide in the United States. *Journal of the American Medical Association: Internal Medicine, 178*(5), 692–700.

Kivisto, A. J. (2015). Male perpetrators of intimate partner homicide: A review and proposed typology. *Journal of the American Academy of Psychiatry and the Law online, 43*(3), 300–312.

Kivisto, A., Ray, B., & Phalen, P. (2017). Firearm legislation and fatal police shootings in the United States. *Public Health Policy, 107*(7), 1068–1075.

Reeping, P., Cerda, M., Kalesan, B., Wiebe, D., Galea, S., & Branas, C. (2019). State gun laws, gun ownership, and mass shootings in the US: cross sectional time series. *The British Medical Journal, 364*(1542), 1–6.

Rosengart, M., Cummings, P., Nathens, A., Heagerty, P., Maier, R., & Rivara, F. (2005). An evaluation of state firearm regulations and homicide and suicide death rates. *Injury Prevention, 11*, 77–83.

Ruddel, R., & Mays, G. (2005). State background checks and firearm homicides. *Journal of Criminal Justice, 33*, 127–136.

Simonetti, J., Rowhani-Rahbar, A., Mills, B., Young, B., & Rivara F. (2015). State firearm legislation and nonfatal firearm injuries. *American Journal of Public Health, 105*(8), 1703–1709.

Siegel, M., & Boine, C. (2019). *What are the most effective policies in reducing gun homicides?* Regional Gun Violence Consortium. Rockefeller Institute of Government.

Steed, R., Moreland, L., & Baker, T. (1990). *The disappearing South? Studies in regional change and continuity.* University of Alabama Press.

8 Fatal Police Violence

The American policing landscape was changed significantly on May 25, 2020, by the horrific and very public death of George Floyd at the hands of City of Minneapolis Police Officer Derek Chauvin. Almost immediately after a cell phone video recording of the event went viral, Americans took to the streets to protest yet another extrajudicial killing of a Black person by the police. The number of Black and other people of color in America experiencing violent policing is difficult to measure as those data are not tracked or reported in a systematic fashion at the national or state level. However, the limited data available strongly suggest that minorities in the United States face disparate and often brutal treatment by police departments across the country (Goff et al., 2016; Pierson et al., 2020). The American Civil Liberties Union (ACLU) estimates 1,000 people annually are killed by the police in America. To put those numbers in context, American police kill people at three times the rate as their peers in Canada and 16 times the rates of Germany and England (ACLU, 2020).

Police killings of Black women, men, and children have historically been the focusing events associated with the call for police reform, a call that has widely been ignored. This chapter will examine police shootings using five years of data derived from *Mapping Police Violence* (MPV). MPV is an advocacy organization that has crowdsourced the most complete database of fatal police encounters available. For the purposes of this chapter, we define a fatal police encounter as:

> an encounter between an on duty or off duty police officer(s) and a community member in which, either accidentally or intentionally while chasing, fighting, arresting, restraining, pepper spraying, using a conductive energy weapon (Taser) or by any other use of force the officer kills a person.
>
> (Mapping Police Violence, 2019; Gaynor et al., 2021)

DOI: 10.4324/9781003134602-8

We use a 50-state comparative design to develop a model that incorporates traditional political, socioeconomic, and firearm legislation to explain the determinants of fatal police encounters. We also utilize a South/non-South model to determine if there are regional differences in the rates of police killings as defined above.

This research is important for several reasons. Although there have been large demonstrations following extrajudicial police killings (most notably, the Michael Brown killing in Ferguson, Missouri, and the Breonna Taylor killing in Louisville, Kentucky), the murder of George Floyd was different because it was widely and directly "witnessed" through a crowdsourced video that was immediately available to anyone who wished to access it. As protest gripped the country, the call for reform was once again front and center. For these reasons we examine fatal police encounters in an effort to better understand officer-involved shootings and how they may vary by region.

We begin this chapter with a review of the existing literature on fatal police violence and present the model for testing. We then turn to a brief discussion of our data sources and methods and proceed to a presentation of the findings of our model. We conclude with some thoughts about the implications of our findings, differences between the South and the non-South, and ideas for future research.

The Challenges of Measuring Police Use of Force

The topic of fatal police violence has been much discussed lately, but few solutions have emerged. Policing is one of only two state or local government functions (corrections is the other) that is defined by the ability of its institutions to carry out the coerciveness of the state. The public expects police to use force when it is necessary to do so; this is what separates policing from other roles of the state (Engel et al., 2020). However, what is unusual is the lack of any national or state-level database cataloging police use of force. Currently, there are several databases that are crowdsourced or compiled by reporters. *The Guardian*, *The Washington Post*, *Mapping Police Violence*, and *KilledbyPolice.net* are the most widely used (Engel et al., 2020; Sherman, 2018; Zimring, 2017). Engel et al. (2020) argue the three most remarkable discoveries from these databases are: over half of fatal police shootings occur in jurisdictions with fewer than 50,000 residents; in almost half of the fatal police shootings the victim had no firearm; when benchmarked against the national population, Black people were 2.3 times more likely to be killed than White people (Engel et al., 2020; Sherman, 2018; Zimring, 2017). It should be noted that the most constricting limitation on this database is it does not account for the dynamics of the interaction that resulted in the fatal outcome. Although the details of the encounter are captured in the narrative section of the official police report, that narrative is from the perspective of the reporting officer and can be biased, incomplete, or otherwise flawed. The most widely accepted remedy for this limitation is the systematic social observation of the incident (Goff et al., 2016); unfortunately, this is not practical for this research. Therefore, this analysis will not address situational factors.

A great deal of the literature concerning fatal police violence has centered on the demographic characteristics of the victims; to date, there has been little research to determine the state-level factors that might influence the propensity of fatal police violence within a state. The risk of being killed by police for people of all races and ethnicities peaks for those between 20 and 35 years of age, with police use of force as a leading cause of death for those between 25 and 29 (Edwards et al., 2019; Wu, 2020). Black and non-White people "face a nontrivial lifetime risk of being killed by police" (Edwards et al., 2019, p. 16793). Nix et al. (2017) suggest that Black people who were shot by police are twice as likely to be unarmed as White people. Conversely, there is a great amount of research that suggests demographic characteristics of the police officers themselves, or their commanders, are significant in predicting police violence. Wu (2020) used the *Washington Post* dataset to examine whether the race of the police chief impacted the number of fatal police shootings. Using the 100 most populated cities as his sample population and controlling for access to a trauma center, crime rates, the demographics of sworn officers, and demographics of the community, the data suggest that police departments with Black chiefs have a statistically significant lower number of fatal shootings than those departments led by White chiefs. Wu (2020) argues that police policies and culture can be greatly influenced by police leadership, in that Black chiefs may value de-escalation or other training that emphasizes alternatives to the use of deadly force.

Studies that examined the race of the officers involved in fatal police shootings have produced mixed results. Using data compiled from 186 officer-involved shootings in the Riverside, California County Sheriff's Office, McElvain and Kposowa (2008) argue that White, non-Hispanic officers are more likely to be involved in police shootings than Hispanic officers, although there were no significant differences between Hispanic officers and Black officers on this dimension. This study also found that male officers were more likely to be involved in shootings than their female counterparts; and officers who have shot their guns in a confrontation previously are more likely to be involved in future shootings. Those officers with college degrees were statistically less likely to be involved in police shootings than those with less education. Lastly, age was significant: the older an officer was, the less likely they were to be involved in a police shooting.

In a 2016 study of police-involved shootings in the New York City Police Department, Ridgeway (2020) had similar findings as McElvain and Kposowa (2008), in that older officers were less likely to be involved in a shooting. Ridgeway (2020) also argues officers who have been disciplined for problematic behavior are more likely to be involved in a shooting. However, contrary to McElvain and Kposowa, this study suggests Black officers are statistically more likely to be involved in a shooting than White officers.

Considering factors other than demographics, Nagin (2020) argues there is a strong relationship between firearm availability and fatal police shootings. Since there is no formal accounting of firearm availability at the state level the researcher uses the number of suicides by firearm as a proxy. This is a widely used and validated measure found in the academic literature (Cook & Ludwig, 2006). Interestingly, Nagin (2020) suggests not only is there a strong statistically significant relationship between states with higher rates of firearm availability on fatal police encounters, but there is also a statistically significant relationship between fatal police encounters with unarmed people. Nagin (2020) suggests that police perceive they are at greater risk in those states with high firearm availability and may be quicker to use fatal force – even when the person turns out to be unarmed.

Using Metropolitan Statistical Areas (MSAs) as their unit of analysis Schwartz and Jahn (2020) examined fatal police violence. Their research suggests across all MSAs Black people were 3.23 times more likely to be killed by the police compared to White and Latinx populations. However, they found a wide geographic variation in the occurrence of fatal police violence. MSAs in the West and Southwest have the highest number while MSAs in the Northeast and Midwest have the lowest overall rates of fatal police violence. The deadliest MSA is Anniston–Oxford–Jacksonville, Alabama, which had nine times the annual rate of fatal police violence compared to the least, the Buffalo–Cheektowaga–Niagara Falls, New York (MSA).

Using the data from MPV Project, Gaynor et al. (2021) chose to narrow down fatal police encounters to just Black victims in the 100 largest cities in the United States. These researchers included an independent variable that measured for former Confederate states. They examined the rate of Black women, men, and children killed by police in cities with a population greater than 100,000 people. Their model confirms prior research in that Black people are killed by police disproportionately. Additionally, controlling for crime rates, the research suggests race and segregation are statistically significant indicators of fatal police encounters. More specifically, Black people are killed by police at a higher rate within Black communities, when Black people live in what are traditionally White neighborhoods, they are killed at rates that are significantly (statistically) lower. These researchers argue "their proximity to whiteness may offer increased security that those who live in Black spaces do not have" (p.61). This research also included a South/non-South variable that was not significant under the studied circumstances.

Limitations of Existing Datasets

A common thread across most research concerning fatal police violence is the lack of availability and reliability of appropriate data. Currently, there is no national database maintained by the Federal Bureau of Investigation (FBI) or any other federal agency that accurately tracks the number of people that are victims of fatal police violence in the United States (Matusiak et al., 2020; Wu, 2020). The FBI (2019) did, however, recently begin to collect use of force data that includes fatal police violence, but law enforcement agencies have the option to opt out of the program. The lack of valid, reliable data has impacted researchers from across disciplines in assessing the societal impact of fatal police encounters – and has also hindered the ability of researchers to inform practice when it comes to making data-driven public policy decisions (and to hold police departments accountable for their behaviors) (Kane, 2007; Matusiak et al., 2020). In the absence of an official database, researchers have to fall back on crowdsourced data collected by media sources (Campbell et al., 2018; Nix et al., 2017). At the national level, employees at the *Washington Post* have crowdsourced data from media outlets, government websites, social media outlets and police oversight groups to develop the most comprehensive database of fatal police encounters starting in 2015 (Tate et al., 2016).

Modeling Fatal Police Violence

There is substantial evidence that suggests a relationship between the demographics of the community members and fatal police encounters (Edwards et al., 2019; Nix et al., 2017; Wu, 2020). There also is data to support that Black and people of color between the ages of 20 and 35 are more likely to be victims of fatal police encounters (Edwards et al., 2019). In addition to the common predictors, we include several variables not found frequently in the literature concerning fatal police encounters; these variables are indicators of how states implement policies in order to maintain social control of Black, other persons of color, and additional vulnerable members of the population (Kenter et al., 2020; Soss et al., 2001). We suspect that those political decisions will spill over into the actions of street-level bureaucrats – in this case, police officers.

Operational Definitions

The dependent variable for this research is the number of fatal police encounters between 2013 and 2018 at the state level and these data come from the Mapping Police Violence project (2019). In attempting to explain police violence we employ several contextual, or need variables, in addition to the baseline model.

Universal Background Checks

Most firearms are initially purchased through a federally licensed dealer. Therefore, the initial purchase of a new firearm requires a background check to confirm the purchaser has not been disqualified from lawfully purchasing and possessing a firearm. States have the choice to further legislate universal background checks for all firearm transactions not governed by federal regulations. Universal background checks for the purchase of firearms at the state level have been found to reduce firearm-related homicides by nearly ten percent (Siegel & Boine, 2019). States that control access to firearms in this manner have a better chance of preventing the misuse of those firearms which in turn would decrease fatal police encounters.

Concealed Carry Permitting ("May Issue" Laws)

The decision to regulate who qualifies for a concealed carry permit or if a permit is required to carry a concealed firearm is a state decision. Some states do not regulate concealed carry of firearms and allow those citizens who are lawfully possessing a firearm to carry it concealed if they choose. Some states require a citizen to apply for a concealed carry permit with an automatic approval if the person is qualified to possess a firearm. Those states that have legislated to give law enforcement authorities discretion when approving concealed carry permits are referred to "may issue" laws. Siegel and Boine's (2019) research argues that those states have fewer firearm-related homicides than states that do not have that law.

Violent Misdemeanors

Federal legislation mandates people who have been convicted of a felony and those convicted of domestic assault be disqualified from possessing firearms. However, states have the option of legislating further restrictions on who can lawfully possess firearms within that state. States that consider violent misdemeanor convictions as a disqualifier for firearm possession have a 19.3% reduction in firearm-related homicides (Siegel & Boine,

2019). We expect states with this law will have fewer fatal police encounters. Table 8.1 displays the descriptive statistics for the variables employed in this model.

Analysis

In an attempt to better understand and explain officer-involved shootings and the use of deadly force across the country we ran three different models: the 50-state baseline; the non-South; and the South (see Table 8.2). The findings across each are fascinating and highlight the disparity of perception and region. In the 50-state baseline model, there are five strongly significant predictors of officer-involved shootings. Poverty and minority population come as little surprises, but the direction is unexpected. This finding is in line with the existing literature that suggests Black and other persons of color are the victims of fatal police encounters in disproportionate numbers, despite there being fewer overall police shootings in the majority of these states.

Less surprisingly, education, violent offender restrictions, and "may issue" laws behave as expected. In states with a higher educated populace, we find a statistically significant decrease in officer-involved shootings. States with "may issue" laws also have a significant negative relationship with officer-involved shootings, while more severe violent offender restrictions lead to increased officer-involved shootings across the 50-state baseline model.

In the non-South model, the results are largely the same, with minor degree variation and one interesting change. In the non-South, Republican gubernatorial control is a significant predictor of decreased officer-involved shootings, bringing a partisan element into what would generally be

Table 8.1   Descriptive Statistics: Fatal Police Violence

	Obsv	Mean	SD	Min	Max
Dependent variable	300	21.72	28.67	0	200
Republican gubernatorial control	350	.62	.49	0	1
Republican legislative control	343	.59	.49	0	1
Poverty	350	10.27	2.84	4	19.2
Minority	350	20.08	11.43	3	57.7
Unemployment	350	6.96	2.21	2.6	13.1
Education	350	88.49	3.07	81.1	93.5
Universal background checks	350	.18	.39	0	1
Violent offender restrictions	350	.10	.30	0	1
"May issue" laws	350	.19	.39	0	1
South	350	.22	.41	0	1

Table 8.2 Regression Results: Fatal Police Violence

	Baseline Regression	Non-South	South
Republican gubernatorial	−.55	−8.03*	14.23*
control	(3.36)	(4.01)	(8.24)
Republican legislative control	4.10	5.85	Omitted
	(3.85)	(4.04)	
Poverty	−5.10***	−4.99***	−3.85
	(1.18)	(1.42)	(2.70)
Minority	−5.44***	−.46*	−1.75***
	(.19)	(.22)	(.49)
Unemployment	−.84	−1.33	−1.75
	(.97)	(1.14)	(2.19)
Education	−9.11***	−25.94***	−10.09***
	(1.07)	(3.51)	(2.74)
Universal background checks	5.30	−.74	Omitted
	(4.64)	(5.13)	
Violent offender restrictions	40.49***	38.70***	Omitted
	(7.02)	(7.23)	
"May issue" laws	−21.27***	−21.39***	Omitted
	(6.14)	(6.45)	
South	5.38		
	(5.01)		
Constant	893.18***	85.42***	999.45***
	(106.01)	(15.34)	(255.36)
R^2	.37	.38	.38
N=	294	204	66

Note: Standard errors in parentheses. Levels of statistical significance: * 0.1; **0.05; *** 0.01. Bold coefficients indicate a significant difference at the 0.1 level in the effects for non-South versus South.

considered a nonpartisan issue. All other significant variables from the baseline model remain in the same overall direction and general significance between the 50-state and non-South models.

Examining the South, we find the results diverge greatly in terms of predicting officer-involved shootings than in the prior two models. In the South, once again, partisanship matters, just in the opposite direction. Republican gubernatorial control predicts greater officer-involved shootings. There is some expected distortion here. Modeling state leadership in a hyper-local issue, it is difficult to ascertain the true impact of the chief executive, yet the literature tells us that conservative leadership is generally pro-gun and advocates for lesser gun ownership restrictions.

Minority population and education are each significant in the same directions as the prior two models but, interestingly, poverty is no longer a significant predictor. Perhaps most striking is what happens to the contextual variables in the model. In our sample time frame, from 2012 to 2018, there is effectively no variation within the southern states when it comes to universal background checks, violent offender restrictions, and "may issue" laws. This lack of variation causes the three contextual variables to drop from the model. Further exploration, comparing the difference of mean tests between the contextual variables in the baseline and South models indicates that each of the three variables is significantly different between the non-South and the South.

Discussion/Conclusion

The findings of this chapter highlight the regional differences between the South and non-South concerning fatal police encounters. Republican control of the governor's mansion is significant in the South, indicating the Republican leadership is positively associated with increased officer-involved shootings. The traditional "get tough on crime" rhetoric is often played out in aggressive police tactics, the most aggressive being the extra-judicial killing of a person. In the South model the three pieces of state legislation that significantly contribute to reduced firearm violence – universal background checks, violent offender restrictions, and "may issue" laws – are stagnant, lacking variance to the point they are excluded from the model. Despite the exclusion, the findings (or lack thereof) are interesting nonetheless. The deeply ingrained traditionalistic political culture in the South, the predominance of Republican leadership, and longstanding tradition have created an environment where there is effectively no variation among the contextual predictors. What matters outside of the South does not register in the South, not because the variables are irrelevant, but because the environment is completely different.

The American system of federalism has enabled an arrangement in which there are over 18,000 local law enforcement agencies in the United States operating under very little federal oversight. Individual states have been tasked with creating the framework for agencies that operate within their borders. These frameworks vary widely in terms of training requirements, policies, and accountability. The challenge here is attempting to explain a hyper-local issue at the state level with minimal empirical evidence.

Given the spate of recent fatal police violence, there have been some efforts at reform. Recently proposed federal legislation (H.R. 7120, The George Floyd Justice in Policing Act of 2021) seeks to standardize minimum accountability measures across all 50 states. The law proposes withholding federal funding to state and local law enforcement agencies that do not comply with the elements of the act, such as banning chokeholds and no-knock warrants. The law also mandates specific data collection requirements as well as requiring certain blocks of instruction concerning racial and religious bias. Further, there are sections of the law concerning prosecuting law enforcement officers at the federal level (United States 116 Congress, 2021). At the state level, some efforts have been made to address police reform. Perhaps the most sweeping is New York State's Executive Order 203. Governor Cuomo ordered through an executive order all law enforcement agencies in the state to examine their policies and practices, engage with their Black and Brown communities, and co-produce recommended reform efforts (Cuomo, 2020).

While federal and state legislation is an important step, the implementation of this legislation will be pushed to the local level and will ultimately determine whether we emerge with a more equitable new paradigm in policing or repeat the cycle of injustice and racialized violence that has been embedded in police culture for generations. As gun violence seemingly increases throughout the country and officer-involved shootings routinely make the evening news, there have been increased calls for police reform at all levels of government. Critical to this is better understanding the issue. How prevalent is fatal police violence; how can we better collect this data; what factors drive fatal police violence? This chapter begins the conversation, but to truly address the systematic issues plaguing police use of deadly force, a much more nuanced understanding is needed. Meaningful reform must start with reporting and data collection practices at the local, state, and federal levels.

References

American Civil Liberties Union. (2020). *The other epidemic: Fatal police shootings in the time of Covid-19*. American Civil Liberties Union. https://www.aclu.org/sites/default/files/field_document/aclu_the_other_epidemic_fatal_police_shootings_2020.pdf

Campbell, B.A., Nix, J., & Maguire, E.R. (2018). Is the number of citizens fatally shot by police increasing in the post-Ferguson era? *Crime & Delinquency, 64*(3), 398–420.

Cook, P.J., & Ludwig, J. (2006). The social cost of gun ownership. *Journal of Public Economics, 90*, 379–391.

Cuomo, A. (2020). New York State Governor executive order 203: Police reform and reinvention collaborative. https://www.governor.ny.gov/news/no-203-new-york-state-police-reform-and-reinvention-collaborative

Edwards, F., Lee, H., & Esposito, M. (2019). Risk of being killed by police use of force in the United States by age, race-ethnicity, and sex. *Proceedings of the National Academy of Sciences, 116*(34), 16793–16798.

Engel, R.S., McManus, H.D., & Isaza, G.T. (2020). Moving beyond "best practices": Experiences in police reform and a call for evidence to reduce officer involved shootings. *Annals of the American Academy of Political and Social Sciences,* *687*, 146–165.

Federal Bureau of Investigation. (2019). *National use of force data collections.* https ://www.fbi.gov/services/cjis/ucr/use-of-force

Gaynor, T., Kang, S., & Williams, B. (2021). Segregated spaces and separated races: The relationship between state-sanctioned violence, place, and Black identity. *Journal of the Social Sciences, 7*(1), 50–66.

Goff, P.A., Lloyd, T., Geller, A., Raphael, S., & Glaser, J. (2016). *The science of justice: Race, arrests, and police use of force.* Center for Policing Equity. https ://policingequity.org/what-we-do/research/the-science-of-justice-race-arrests-an d-police-use-of-force

Kane, R.J. (2007). Collect and release data on coercive police actions. *Criminology, 6*(4), 773–780.

Kenter, R.C., Morris, J.C., Mayer, M.K., & Newton, J.M. (2020). Reconsidering state variation in incarceration rates. *Politics & Policy, 48*(6), 1029–1061.

Mapping Police Violence. (2019). About the data. https://mappingpoliceviolence. org/aboutthedata.

Matusiak, M.C., Cavanaugh, M.R., & Stephenson, M. (2020). An assessment of officer-involved shooting data transparency in the United States. *Journal of Interpersonal Violence,* 1–25. https://doi.org/10.1177%2F0886260520913646.

McElvain, Y., & Kposowa, J. (2008). Police officer characteristics and the likelihood of using deadly force. *Criminal Justice and Behavior, 35*(4), 505–521.

Nagin, D.S. (2020). Firearm availability and fatal police shootings. *The Annals of the American Academy of Political and Social Science, 687*(1), 49–57.

Nix, J., Campbell, B.A., Byers, E.H., & Alpert, G.P. (2017). A bird's eye view of civilians killed by police in 2015. *Criminology & Public Policy, 16*, 1–32.

Pierson, E., Simoiu, C., Overgoor, J., Corrbett-Davies, S., Jenson, D., Shoemaker, A., Ramachandron, V., Barghouty, P., Phillips, C., Shroff, R., & Goel, S. (2020). A large-scale analysis of racial disparities in police stops across the United States. *Nature Human Behavior, 4*(7), 736–745.

Ridgeway, G. (2020). The role of individual officer characteristics in police shootings. *Annals of the American Academy of Political Science, 687*(1), 58–66.

Schwartz, G.L., & Jahn, J.L. (2020). Mapping fatal police violence across U.S. metropolitan areas: Overall rates and racial/ethnic inequities, 2013–2017. *PLoS One, 15*(6), 2013-2017.

Sherman, L.W. (2018). Reducing fatal police shootings as systems crashes: Research theory, and practice. *Annual Review of Criminology, 11*(3), 319–334.

Siegel, M., & Boine, C. (2019). *What are the most effective policies in reducing gun homicides?* Regional Gun Violence Consortium. Rockefeller Institute of Government.

Soss, J., Sanford, J., Schram, F., Vartanian, T.P., & O'Brien, E. (2001). Setting the terms of relief: Explaining state policy choices in the devolution revolution. *American Journal of Political Science, 45*(2), 378–395.

Tate, J., Jenkin, J., Rich, S., Muyskens, J., Elliott, K., Mellnik, T., & Williams, A. (2016, July 7). How the *Washington Post* is examining police shootings in the United States. *The Washington Post.* https://www.washingtonpost.com/national/

how-the-washington-post-is-examining-police-shootings-in-the-united-states/
2016/07/07/d9c52238-43ad-11e6-8856-f26de2537a9d_story.html
United States Congress. (2021). House Resolution 7120; The George Floyd Justice
in Policing Act. https://www.congress.gov/bill/116th-congress/house-bill/7120
Wu, S. (2020). Leadership matters: Police chief race and fatal shootings by police
officers. *Social Science Quarterly*, *102*(1), 407–419.
Zimring, F.E. (2017). *When police kill*. Harvard University Press.

9 COVID-19 Pandemic Response

The worldwide outbreak of the novel coronavirus (COVID-19) that began in 2019 was a public health crisis almost unprecedented in the modern era. After the first infections were detected in Wuhan, China, in late 2019, cases quickly began to be detected in other nations around the world; the first official cases in the United States were reported in January 2020. A year later, the death toll in the United States alone had surpassed 400,000[1] (CDC, 2020a), and the number of confirmed infections in the United States had surpassed 18 million. As the pandemic raged, states were faced with the prospect of formulating a response to the crisis and determining how best to protect their citizens from a highly infectious virus with no known cure. At the point that the United States had declared a national health emergency on January 31st, 2020, the virus had taken hold in the United States and many other nations across the world. By early March it became increasingly clear that the virus was spreading rapidly through the population, and the president issued a national state of emergency on March 13th (Whitehouse .gov, 2020). At this point, many states began to institute a series of actions and orders designed to protect citizens from infection and to stop the spread of the virus.

The United States has largely been sheltered from virulent disease outbreaks; the last time the United States saw an outbreak of this scale was the influenza epidemic of 1918–1920 that killed an estimated 675,000 Americans (Crosby, 2003). Much has been learned about both methods to control viral transmission and palliative treatments for pulmonary viruses in the intervening years, but the nation was still largely unprepared to cope with the scale of the COVID-19 pandemic. The initial response to the pandemic at both the national and state levels was confused and was marked by misinformation, disinformation, and active attempts on the part of the Trump administration to downplay the seriousness of the crisis (Woodward, 2020). In the absence of clear federal guidelines, states began individually to take actions to address the pandemic and slow its progression. Governors

DOI: 10.4324/9781003134602-9

issued emergency declarations, ordered school closures, shut businesses, restaurants, and prohibited public gatherings. Some states moved quickly to institute public health protections, while other governors resisted calls to take action. The issue was further confused by the president who, in addition to spreading misinformation about the virus, refused publicly to follow guidance from infectious disease experts (such as mask-wearing) and resisted releasing federal stockpiles of personal protective equipment (PPE) and respiratory ventilators to alleviate critical shortages of these items in states (see Bowling et al., 2020). The net result was a loose patchwork of poorly coordinated actions and decisions by states. As pressure began to build in late April for states to relax restrictions and reopen businesses and schools, the same piecemeal decision-making was repeated. Some states rescinded previous orders, while other states left restrictions in place. As infection and death rates began to rise again in June and July, the cycle repeated itself. The virus paid no attention to state borders.

Anecdotal observations suggest that state governors made choices based largely on partisan affiliation, but a closer examination suggests that the issues were more nuanced (see Williamson et al., 2021). Furthermore, those anecdotal observations would suggest that southern states were more likely to close late, open early, and resist more stringent actions. For example, Republican governor Ron DeSantis of Florida refused to close beaches in the state at the beginning of the pandemic, which coincided with the height of the traditional spring break period (Collinson, 2020; Faulders, Kim, & Rubin, 2020). Governor Brian Kemp (R-GA) sued local governments who took action to institute stricter restrictions than those imposed at the state level (Romo, 2020). At the same time, other states, such as North Dakota, took few precautions at all. Faced with a national pandemic, did southern states differ in their actions in response to the pandemic? Did southern states institute less strict orders; did they impose restrictions later than other states, and did they lift these restrictions earlier than other states?

The purpose of this chapter is to test the proposition that southern states differed from the rest of the nation in terms of their response to the pandemic. As of this writing, three different vaccines have begun to be distributed in the United States, bringing some hope that the spread of the virus can be controlled, and that both infection and death rates will fall. Our analysis focuses on the first five months of the pandemic (March through July) as a means to discern differences in the actions of southern states from the rest of the nation. To this point, there are a few empirical scholarly analyses of state responses to the pandemic, and no studies that examine differences between the South and the rest of the nation. Most of the work to this point has been produced by epidemiologists (see, e.g., Calerdon-Larranaga et al., 2020; Dowd et al., 2020), and seeks to explain infection and death rates.

Our work focuses specifically on state policy actions in response to the pandemic. We employ several variables related to state decisions, including measures of the vulnerability of a state's population, political and partisanship factors, economic indicators, and health and demographic measures. Our goal is to explain state choices in the early months of the pandemic, and to determine whether any policy differences can be detected between southern states and the rest of the nation.

State Actions to Respond to the COVID-19 Pandemic

The confusion and inconsistency in pandemic response from the national government had significant implications for federalism. The lack of inter-jurisdictional coordination left states with no clear guidance about how to react to the pandemic, which led to even higher levels of confusion and economic distress (Haffajee & Mello, 2020), as states struggled to find a balance between public safety and economic damage caused by shut-downs. Much of the early scholarly work addressing concerns of federalism described the resulting action as "chaotic" (Bowling et al., 2020) and "confused" (Kettl, 2020). Policy responses by states varied widely, which led to further confusion on the part of citizens and business owners as they struggled to decipher the rules in different states (Comfort et al., 2020). Following the president's declaration of a national emergency on March 13 the first action taken by most states was to follow suit (Knauer, 2020). This marked the first time in American history when all 50 states were under a disaster declaration (Coleman, 2020). Two days later, the Centers for Disease Control and Prevention (CDC) issued guidelines for restrictions on public gatherings; these were soon instituted in many states (Holcombe & Andone, 2020). These restrictions were quickly followed in some states by additional gubernatorial orders to close restaurants, bars, and schools, along with "stay at home/shelter in place" and social distancing orders. A number of states across the United States modeled their orders on emerging patterns of virus transmission, but there was still substantial variation (Benton, 2020; Kettl, 2020).

In spite of statements by the president to the contrary (Craig & Dennis, 2020), the policy decisions regarding pandemic response are constitutionally in the hands of states and, for the most part, governors of the states. As is the case in many other policy arenas, states still look to the national government for guidance and leadership in times of crisis. States lack the expertise and resources found at the national level and turn to the national government for direction. While other federal systems of government around the world faced similar challenges, in most of those cases issues of public health were placed above partisanship and posturing (Rozell & Wilcox,

2020). Moreover, substantial differences exist between states in terms of their infrastructure, resources, and vulnerability to the pandemic; when coupled with an inherent mistrust of government intervention (Huberfield et al., 2020), the ability of states to respond varied wildly across the nation.

A Model of State Action and Response to the Pandemic

To model state behavior in response to the pandemic, we construct a framework that seeks to explain the actions initiated by states to ameliorate the spread of the virus. We thus create a dependent variable that captures six independent decisions commonly considered by states: emergency declarations, restrictions on bars and restaurants, limits on public gatherings, mask requirements, stay-at-home orders, and quarantine orders. Our dependent variable is an additive index of all six requirements. By capturing data by state-day and recording the date on which orders are issued or rescinded, we can capture the policy drivers of these decisions as they happen. All states thus start with a value of zero. As a state takes an action, the value of its index changes from a zero to a value of one. Each additional restriction in place adds one additional point to the score. Likewise, as states remove restrictions, the state's score is reduced by one point for each restriction removed. The value of the index can thus range from one to six. There is significant variation in this index; some states instituted all six restrictions, while other states instituted only one or two restrictions. States also added and then lifted restrictions during the measurement period.

In order to explain the variation in our dependent variable, we test four different explanations. The first explanation is a political explanation. The casual observer of the pandemic response cannot help but notice that partisan politics played an important role. There are two dimensions to this issue: first, most state actions were instituted through executive powers by the state governor, so we measure the party affiliation of the state governor in 2020. We hypothesize that partisan considerations will make Republican governors less likely to institute initial restrictions, but more likely to lift any restrictions in place earlier than their Democratic colleagues. The second element is a measure of support for the president. Supporters of the president were typically outspoken in their objections to state restrictions, and less likely to comply with restrictions. To measure the level of support for the president in a state, we use the percentage of the vote won by the president in the 2016 election. The more support the president received in 2016, the less likely states will be to institute COVID-19 restrictions.

States differ in terms of the susceptibility of the population to disease. States with a high number of citizens with underlying conditions that make them more susceptible to serious virus complications should be willing to take action to protect their vulnerable citizens. To measure the vulnerability of the population, we employ a state health index developed by the United Health Foundation. Because older Americans are also more vulnerable to the virus (CDC, 2020b), we also measure the percentage of the population 65 years of age and older. Because minority populations are more vulnerable to getting the virus (due to density, lack of health care, etc.) we also include a measure of the percentage of the non-White population in each state. Public health officials warn that the virus spreads more quickly in populated areas, because people are both more numerous and closer together than their rural counterparts. We, therefore, include a measure of population density for each state. Finally, we control for socioeconomic status by including the Gini index of wealth disparity.

Public statements made by elected officials, business owners, and citizens during the pandemic speak to fears about economic distress caused by the shutdown of businesses. Many governors from both parties echoed these fears, and some publicly stated opposition to certain restrictions because of the possibility of economic damage. Moreover, unemployment rates were very different in different states both before and during the pandemic. In Nevada, where gaming drives the economy, the cessation of operations of casinos caused massive unemployment. On the other hand, rural farming states such as Nebraska and South Dakota saw few immediate effects of unemployment. Therefore, it is reasonable to assume that some governors instituted or lifted restrictions in response to rising unemployment. We include a variable that captures the number of weekly new unemployment claims in each state. We posit that states with high unemployment rates are less likely to institute restrictions.

Our third explanation suggests that decisions about restrictions were made in response to rising (or falling) rates of infection and COVID-related deaths in the state. For example, New York experienced a sharp increase in both infections and deaths early in the pandemic, which were followed closely by new restrictions. Conversely, North Dakota had relatively few infections and deaths during the same period, and few restrictions were in place. We thus hypothesize that states experiencing higher rates of infection and deaths will be more likely to add restrictions.

South/Non-South Differences

Southern states tended to be led by Republican governors in 2020. Some of these governors, including Florida governor Ron DeSantis and Georgia governor Brian Kemp, were both publicly supportive of the president and against the imposition of statewide restrictions to prevent spread of the virus (see Collinson, 2020). However, southern states tend to have populations that are more vulnerable to the virus than other states, and the infection and death rates in some states were higher than the national average. So, while southern states were perhaps the most vulnerable to the virus, political factors were also clearly important in determining state actions.

But, were these factors strong enough to make the South different as a region from the rest of the nation? We posit that southern states are less likely to institute restrictions, and more likely to more quickly remove restrictions they do impose, than non-South states. We also expect that measures of community vulnerability do not explain restriction decisions, but economic concerns (unemployment claims) do help predict state decisions. We also expect that death rates, but not infection rates, contribute to the variation in state decisions.

Data and Methods

Data for our dependent variable are drawn from Fullman et al. (2020). As noted earlier, we code both the action taken by the state, and capture the date of the action as well. The value of the dependent variable thus changes by day as the number of actions changes. The value of the dependent variable for each observation varies from 0 (for no actions taken) to 6 (all actions taken). Data for gubernatorial party control are drawn from Ballotpedia (2020), and data on the percentage of votes in a state for Trump in 2016 are from the American Presidency Project (2020).

Our measures of population vulnerability (percent population older than 65; percent of non-White citizens in the state; and the state's Gini index) are all drawn from the American Community Survey (US Census, 2020). The health index variable is a state-level measure from the United Health Foundation (2020) and represents 2019 rankings (the most recent data available). Population density is derived by using the 2019 state population estimates from the American Community Survey and dividing by the land area of the state in square miles. Data for infections and deaths from the virus are reported by day and are from data reported by *The New York Times* (2020). These values are lagged in our models, as described later in this chapter. Finally, new unemployment claims are taken from weekly data available from the US Bureau of Labor Statistics (2020) and are seasonally adjusted.

Our unit of analysis is state-day, which provides a dataset with 7,650 observations for the study period. We begin the study period on March 1, 2020, roughly two weeks prior to the national declaration of emergency, and end the period on July 31, 2020. Data are analyzed using Stata version 16, and we employ logistic regression techniques to estimate all of the models except for the index models, for which we employ ordinal regression. Table 9.1 presents the descriptive statistics for the variables in our model.

Table 9.1   Descriptive Statistics: COVID-19 Response

	Obsv	Mean	Sd	Min	Max
Index	7,650	4.33	1.70	0	7
Lagged infections	7,379	437.15	496.43	.01	2,506.35
Lagged deaths	7,379	18.99	30.95	0	178.17
Lagged claims	7,643	.68	.63	.02	3.90
Republican governor	7,650	.52	.50	0	1
Trump vote	7,650	49.26	10.19	30.04	68.5
Population density	7,650	200.75	262.79	1.29	1,207.69
Population older than 65	7,650	15.64	1.80	10.52	19.73
Non-White	7,650	23.31	12.62	5.51	75
Gini	7,650	.46	.02	.42	.51
Health index	7,650	.02	.50	−1.01	.85
South	7,650	.22	.41	0	1

Analysis

We begin with an examination of a 50-state baseline model (see Table 9.2). Of immediate interest are the largely negative relationships between a number of different independent and control variables and individual state choices. For example, the infection rate is negatively associated with all state actions other than the mask mandate, and Republican governors are also much less likely to enact all restrictions other than a state of emergency declaration and quarantine orders. The percentage of 2016 Trump voters is also negatively associated with the imposition of state restrictions. Likewise, a state's Gini index is negatively related to all but the quarantine element. Looking at the index variable, unemployment claims, infections, and deaths are significant, although Republican governor and Trump vote are not. Finally, the South dummy variable fails to reach significance in the index model.

For the non-South model (see Table 9.3) the pattern is similar to the baseline model. Infections are negatively associated with state restrictions, although non-South states tend to be responsive to death rates. The political variables tend to be significant, particularly in the case of state actions that might be construed to limit personal freedom (e.g., limits on gatherings, mask mandates). The other notable element in this model is the relative significance of the variables that represent measures of the vulnerability of the population. However, for most variables, the coefficients are negative, suggesting that a greater level of vulnerability does not drive state action to limit the spread of the virus. For the index variable, the only positively associated and statistically significant variable is unemployment claims. However, the positive association seems to flip our expectations, in that more unemployment is associated with more restrictions. Given the public

Table 9.2 Baseline Regression Results: COVID-19 Response

	State Of Emergency	Gathering Limit	Bar Restrict.	Dining Restrict.	Stay Home	Mask Mandate	Quarantine	Index
Lagged infections	-.01**	-.01**	-.01**	-.01**	-.01**	.01**	-.01	-.01**
	(.01)	(.01)	(.01)	(.01)	(.01)	(.01)	(.01)	(.01)
Lagged deaths	.02**	.04**	.02**	.02**	.03**	.03**	.01	.02**
	(.01)	(.01)	(.01)	(.01)	(.01)	(.01)	(.01)	(.01)
Lagged claims	7.53**	2.69**	2.86**	2.73**	2.14**	-.97**	.10*	9.68**
	(.54)	(.14)	(.17)	(.16)	(.07)	(.08)	(.05)	(.64)
Republican governor	.42**	-.73**	-.30**	-.34**	-.82**	-1.16**	.26**	.32
	(.16)	(.10)	(.10)	(.11)	(.07)	(.09)	(.06)	(.17)
Trump vote	-.03*	-.09**	-.06**	-.07**	-.05**	-.14**	.04**	-.01
	(.01)	(.01)	(.01)	(.01)	(.01)	(.01)	(.01)	(.01)
Population density	.01	.01**	-.01	-.01	.01	.01**	-.01*	.01**
	(.01)	(.01)	(.01)	(.01)	(.01)	(.01)	(.01)	(.01)
Population older than 65	-.07	.05*	.20**	.21**	-.01	.22**	.24**	-.10*
	(.04)	(.02)	(.02)	(.02)	(.02)	(.02)	(.02)	(.04)
Non-White	-.01	-.04**	-.06**	-.06**	.01	.01*	.01**	-.02*
	(.01)	(.01)	(.01)	(.01)	(.01)	(.01)	(.01)	(.01)
Gini	-19.89**	-36.49**	-1.63	-5.10	-8.18**	-24.04**	5.41*	-10.01*
	(4.75)	(3.21)	(3.50)	(3.42)	(2.47)	(3.11)	(2.18)	(5.08)
Health index	-.56*	-1.36**	.18	-.02	-.17	-1.39**	1.51**	-.16
	(.23)	(.13)	(.14)	(.13)	(.12)	(.15)	(.09)	(.23)
South	.25	1.80**	1.60**	1.47**	.45**	.29*	-.68**	.10
	(.22)	(.13)	(.15)	(.15)	(.11)	(.13)	(.10)	(.23)
Constant	13.38**	21.90**	2.96	4.71**	4.54**	12.78**	-9.22**	8.57**
	(2.39)	(1.61)	(1.72)	(1.69)	(1.30)	(1.72)	(1.10)	(2.53)
Pseudo r²	.31	.27	.20	.19	.30	.41	.08	.35
Log likelihood	-1,014.51	-2,514.07	-2,146.88	-2,207.24	-3,268.55	-2,539.63	-4,309.11	-915.75
N =	7,379	7,379	7,379	7,379	7,379	7,379	7,379	7,379

Note: Standard errors in parentheses. Levels of statistical significance: * 0.05; ** 0.01.

Table 9.3 Non-South Regression Results: COVID-19 Response

	State Of Emergency	Gathering Limit	Bar Restrict.	Dining Restrict.	Stay Home	Mask Mandate	Quarantine	Index
Lagged infections	-.01**	-.01**	-.01**	-.01**	-.01**	-.01	-.01	-.01**
	(.01)	(.01)	(.01)	(.01)	(.01)	(.01)	(.01)	(.01)
Lagged deaths	.04**	.05**	.03**	.03**	.03**	.05**	.01	.02**
	(.01)	(.01)	(.01)	(.01)	(.01)	(.01)	(.01)	(.01)
Lagged claims	5.98**	2.32**	2.57**	2.48**	1.87**	-.93**	.07	9.10**
	(.57)	(.14)	(.16)	(.15)	(.07)	(.09)	(.05)	(.70)
Republican governor	.45*	-.53**	-.15	-.25*	-.62**	-1.47**	-.07	.33
	(.18)	(.11)	(.17)	(.16)	(.08)	(.10)	(.06)	(.18)
Trump vote	-.03**	-.10**	-.07**	-.08**	-.05**	-.14**	.06**	-.02
	(.01)	(.01)	(.01)	(.01)	(.01)	(.09)	(.01)	(.01)
Population density	7.01e-06	.01**	-.01*	-.01	-.01	.01**	-.01**	.01
	(.01)	(.01)	(.01)	(.01)	(.01)	(.01)	(.01)	(.01)
Population older than 65	-.13**	.19**	.21**	.24**	.01	.32**	.33**	-.11*
	(.05)	(.03)	(.03)	(.03)	(.02)	(.03)	(.02)	(.04)
Non-White	-.01	-.05**	-.06**	-.06**	.01**	.01	.02**	-.02*
	(.01)	(.01)	(.01)	(.01)	(.01)	(.01)	(.01)	(.01)
Gini	-25.45**	-39.33**	-.01	-5.71	-3.26	-28.63**	-2.88	-13.38**
	(5.10)	(3.36)	(3.44)	(3.35)	(2.33)	(3.21)	(2.15)	(5.13)
Health index	-.67**	-1.14**	.30*	.16	-.40**	-1.36**	1.45**	-.03
	(.25)	(.14)	(.14)	(.14)	(.12)	(.17)	(.10)	(.25)
Constant	17.57**	21.87**	2.52	5.24**	1.82	13.55**	-7.66**	10.68**
	(2.63)	(1.66)	(.14)	(1.63)	(1.21)	(1.77)	(.10)	(2.50)
Pseudo r²	.29	.29	.22	.22	.26	.47	.07	.34
Log likelihood	-808.52	-1,983.17	-1,791.76	-1,821.38	-2,893.21	-1,912.19	-3,726.09	-756.05
N =	5,761	5,761	5,761	5,761	5,761	5,761	5,761	5,761

Note: Standard errors in parentheses. Levels of statistical significance: * 0.05; ** 0.01.

statements of many governors that restrictions were putting people out of work, it does not appear that states were particularly responsive to increasing unemployment.

Finally, Table 9.4 presents the same set of models for just the southern states. Our results suggest that southern states in particular were not influenced by the vulnerability of their populations to the virus; few of the related coefficients are significant, and for those that are, most are negative. On the other hand, the effect of politics becomes apparent, in that having a Republican governor decreases the likelihood that these restrictions are adopted. The same holds true for our Trump vote variable. As was the case with non-southern states, southern states were not especially sensitive to infections or deaths; to the extent these variables matter, they tend to be negatively related. The overall pattern, as reflected by the index model, follows a pattern similar to non-South states, although it is also the case that southern states were less sensitive to the vulnerability of their populations.

Discussion/Conclusion

The findings in this model highlight several interesting findings regarding state responses to the pandemic (Table 9.5). While the number of infections had little impact on state decision-making, the number of deaths did – but in different ways. For non-South states, a rising death toll tended to lead to increased restrictions, but in southern states the opposite was true. While the push to remove restrictions and reopen was strong across the country, it was particularly strong in the South. For instance, the Georgia governor resisted a mask mandate, and even went as far as to seek a court injunction against the City of Atlanta, which had instituted a mask mandate (Romo, 2020). The Florida governor resisted efforts to close public beaches (Faulders et al., 2020). Compliance with mask mandates, when instituted in southern states, were generally less effective than in other regions of the country (Henton, 2020).

The effect of having a Republican governor is particularly clear when comparing the South with the non-South. For non-South states, having a Republican governor has a positive, although not significant, impact on the overall index. For southern states, having a Republican governor has a strong and negative impact on the index value. While all states tended to ignore population vulnerability as a factor in their restriction decisions, the coefficients for these variables are higher for southern states than their non-South counterparts. A comparison of means of the index variable indicates a significant difference between the South and the non-South, providing additional arguments for southern distinctiveness in this policy area (see Collinson, 2020).

Table 9.4 South Regression Results: COVID-19 Response

	State Of Emergency	Gathering Limit	Bar Restrict.	Dining Restrict.	Stay Home	Mask Mandate	Quarantine	Index
Lagged infections	-.01**	-.01*	-.01	.01	-.01**	.01**	-.01*	-.01**
	(.01)	(.01)	(.01)	(.01)	(.01)	(.01)	(.01)	(.01)
Lagged deaths	-.01**	-.02**	-.04**	-.03**	.01	-.05**	-.01	-.04**
	(.01)	(.01)	(.01)	(.01)	(.01)	(.01)	(.02)	(.01)
Lagged claims	6.89**	10.83**	11.93**	9.21**	6.64**	-1.65**	1.49**	14.21**
	(.78)	(.88)	(.93)	(.75)	(.46)	(.34)	(.21)	(1.65)
Republican governor	-.44	-2.29**	-1.00**	-1.24**	-1.94**	-4.10**	(omitted)	-1.29*
	(.28)	(.37)	(.36)	(.33)	(.41)	(.97)		(.60)
Trump vote	-.08	.22*	.16*	.10	.50**	-.38	-.44**	-.18
	(.06)	(.08)	(.08)	(.07)	(.09)	(.25)	(.05)	(.12)
Population density	.01	-.01	.01	-.01	.06**	-.06**	-.01*	.01
	(.01)	(.01)	(.01)	(.01)	(.01)	(.01)	(.01)	(.01)
Population older than 65	-.05	-.30	.04	.19	-2.01**	-.09	-.25	-.04
	(.14)	(.19)	(.19)	(.17)	(.25)	(.49)	(.20)	(.28)
Non-White	-.07*	.01	.05	-.01	.29**	.14**	-.44**	-.14*
	(.03)	(.04)	(.04)	(.03)	(.04)	(.02)	(.04)	(.06)
Gini	-.46*	-.62*	-.05	.06	-.99**	-1.05	1.42**	-.67
	(.20)	(.26)	(.26)	(.23)	(.36)	(.67)	(.16)	(.40)
Health index	-2.98*	.70	1.52	.88	.22	(omitted)	(omitted)	-6.04*
	(1.37)	(1.87)	(1.86)	(1.59)	(1.73)			(2.89)
Constant	76.04*	89.23	-2.66	-17.10	132.74	186.64	-183.21**	115.34
	(32.54)	(42.48)	(42.97)	(38.54)	(57.88)	(95.59)	(22.79)	(67.15)
Pseudo r²	.52	.51	.46	.40	.72	.52	.51	.54
Log likelihood	-153.18	-290.33	-273.43	-324.34	-273.30	-343.30	-359.14	-146.65
N=	1,618	1,618	1,618	1,618	1,618	1,618	1,618	1,618

Note: Standard errors in parentheses. Levels of statistical significance: * 0.05; ** 0.01.

Table 9.5 Index Regression Results by Model: COVID-19 Results

	Baseline	Non-South	South
Lagged infections	−.01**	−.01**	−.01**
	(.01)	(.01)	(.01)
Lagged deaths	.02**	.02**	−.04**
	(.01)	(.01)	(.01)
Lagged claims	9.68**	9.10**	14.21**
	(.64)	(.70)	(1.65)
Republican governor	.32	.33	−1.29*
	(.17)	(.18)	(.60)
Trump vote	−.01	−.02	−.18
	(.01)	(.01)	(.12)
Population density	.01**	.01	.01
	(.01)	(.01)	(.01)
Population older than 65	−.10*	−.11*	−.04
	(.04)	(.04)	(.28)
Non-White	−.02*	−.02*	−.14*
	(.01)	(.01)	(.06)
Gini	−10.01*	−13.38**	−.67
	(5.08)	(5.13)	(.40)
Health index	−.16	−.03	−6.04*
	(.23)	(.25)	(2.89)
South	.10		
	(.23)		
Constant	8.57**	10.68**	115.34
	(2.53)	(2.50)	(67.15)
Pseudo r^2	.35	.34	.54
Log likelihood	−915.75	−756.05	−146.65
N=	7,379	5,761	1,618

Note: Standard errors in parentheses. Levels of statistical significance: * 0.05; ** 0.01.

***The index dependent variable is significantly different from the baseline model to the South model at .01.

The states, and the national government, were caught unprepared for the pandemic when it first took hold in early 2020. Lacking clear national leadership (see Lipton et al., 2020), states were left to fend for themselves as they struggled to come to grips with the unfolding catastrophe. As of this writing in late March 2021, more than 550,000 fatalities across the nation have been attributed to COVID-19 and its variants. As a group, southern states were less willing to impose restrictions than the rest of the nation, in spite of having a larger share of at-risk populations. Party politics, coupled with fears of government overreach and intrusion into personal liberties, led to an environment in which personal liberty mattered more than public health and safety. In many ways, this situation reflects the culture of the South (see Cooper & Knotts, 2017).

Note

1   As of this writing in April 2021, the death toll from COVID-19 is over 600,000 in the United States, and total reported infections are over 20 million (CDC, 2020a).

References

American Presidency Project. (2020). 2016 election results. https://www.presiden cy.ucsb.edu/statistics/elections/2016.

Ballotpedia. (2020). List of governors of the American states. https://ballotpedia.org /List_of_governors_of_the_American_states.

Benton, J. (2020). Challenges to federalism and intergovernmental relations and takeaways amid the COVID-19 experience. *American Review of Public Administration, 50*(6–7), 536–542.

Bowling, C.J., Fisk, J.M., & Morris, J.C. (2020). Seeking patterns in chaos: Transactional federalism in the Trump administration's response to the COVID-19 pandemic. *American Review of Public Administration, 50*(6–7), 512–518.

Bureau of Labor Statistics. (2020). Unemployment rates for states. https://www.bls .gov/web/laus/laumstrk.htm.

Calderón-Larrañaga, A., Dekhtyar, S., Vetrano, D.L., Bellander, T., & Fratiglioni, L. (2020). COVID-19: Risk accumulation among biologically and socially vulnerable older populations. *Ageing Research Reviews*, 101149.

Centers for Disease Control and Prevention (CDC). (2020a). CDC COVID data tracker. 15 December 2020. https://covid.cdc.gov/covid-data-tracker/#cases_de athsper100klast7days.

Centers for Disease Control and Prevention (CDC). (2020b). Health equity considerations and racial and ethnic minority groups. 24 July 2020. https://cdc .gov/coronavirus/2019-ncov/community/health-equity/race-ethnicity.html.

Coleman, J. (2020). All 50 states under disaster declaration for first time in US history. *The Hill*. https://thehill.com/policy/healthcare/public-global-health/4 92433-all-50-states-under-disaster-declaration-for-first.

Collinson, S. (2020, April 22). Divisions on battling coronavirus deepen as Trump and southern states push opening. *CNN*. https://www.cnn.com/2020/04/22/poli tics/donald-trump-coronavirus-economy/index.html

Comfort, L., Kapucu, N., Ko, K., Menoni, S., & Siciliano, M. (2020). Crisis decision making on a global scale. *Public Administration Review, 80*(4), 616–622.

Cooper, C.A., & Knotts, H.G. (2017). *The resilience of southern identity: Why the South still matters in the minds of its people*. University of North Carolina Press.

Craig, T., & Dennis, B. (2020). Governors consider lifting virus restrictions; Trump says he alone will decide. *Washington Post*, April 13, 2020. https://www .washingtonpost.com/politics/   governors-form-groups-to-explore-lifting-viru s-restrictions-   trump-says-he-alone-will-decide/2020/04/13/f04a401e-7d84- 11ea-a3ee-13e1ae0a3571_story.html.

Crosby, A. (2003). *America's forgotten pandemic: The influenza of 1918*. Cambridge University Press.

Dowd, J., Andriano, L., Brazel, D., Rotondi, V., Block, P., Ding, X., Liu, Y., & Mills, M. (2020). Demographic science aids in understanding the spread and fatality rates of COVID-19. *Proceedings of the National Academy of Sciences, 117*(18), 9696–9698.

Faulders, K., Kim, S., & Rubin, O. (2020, April 1). After talk with Trump, Florida reverses course on coronavirus stay- at-home order. *ABC-News*. https://abcnews .go.com/Health/ talk-trump-florida-reverses-coronavirus-stay-home-order/ story?id=69926173

Fullman, N., Bang-Jensen, B., Reinke, G., Magistro, B., Castellano, R., Erickson, M., Walcott, R., Dapper, C., Amano, K., Wilkerson, J., & Adolph, C. (2020) State-level social distancing policies in response to COVID-19 in the US. Version 1.118, February 24, 2021. http://www.covid19statepolicy.org

Haffajee, R., & Mello, M. (2020). Thinking globally, acting locally—The US response to Covid-19. *The New England Journal of Medicine, 382*, 75.

Henten, H. (2020). The Northeast leads the country in mask-wearing. *CNN*. https ://www.cnn.com/2020/06/26/politics/maskwearing-coronavirus-analysis/index .html

Holcombe, M., & Andone, D. (2020). The CDC recommends organizers cancel or postpone events with 50 or more people for 8 weeks. *CNN*. https://www.cnn .com/2020/03/15/health/us-coronavirus-sunday-updates/index.html

Huberfeld, N., Gordon, S., & Jones, D. (2020). Federalism complicates the response to the Covid-19 health and economic crisis: What can be done? *Journal of Health Politics, Policy, and Law, 45*(6), 951–965.

Kettl, D. (2020). States divided: The implications of American federalism for Covid-19. *Public Administration Review, 80*(4), 595–602.

Knauer, N. (2020). The Covid-19 pandemic and federalism: Who decides? *N.Y.U. Journal of Legislation and Public Policy, 23*(1), 1–33.

Lipton, E., Sanger, D.E., Haberman, M., Shear, M., Mazzetti, M., & Barnes, J. (2020, April). He could have seen what was coming: Behind Trump's failure on the virus. *New York Times*. https://www.nytimes.com/2020/04/11/us/politics/cor onavirus- trump-response.html

New York Times. (2020). Coronavirus (Covid-19) data in the United States. https:// github.com/nytimes/covid-19-data.

Romo, V. (2020, July 16). Georgia Gov. Brian Kemp sues Atlanta Mayor Keisha Lance bottoms over face mask order. *NPR*. https://www.npr.org/sections/corona virus-live-updates/2020/07/16/892109883/georgia-gov-brian-kemp-sues-atlanta -mayor-keisha-lance-bottoms-over-face-mask-or.

Rozell, M., & Wilcox, C. (2020). Federalism in a time of plague: How federal systems cope with pandemic. *American Review of Public Administration, 50*(6–7), 519–525.

United Health Foundation. 2020. *America's heath rankings: Annual report 2019*. https://www.americashealthrankings.org/learn/reports/2019-annual-report.

U.S. Census. (2020). Social explorer data. https://www.socialexplorer.com.

Whitehouse.gov. (2020). Proclamation on declaring a national emergency concerning the Novel Coronavirus disease (COVID-19) outbreak. https://ww

w.whitehouse.gov/presidential-actions/proclamation-declaring-national-emerg ency-concerning-novel-coronavirus-disease-covid-19-outbreak/.

Williamson, R., Morris, J., Mayer, M., & Hume, J. (2021). Explaining state Coronavirus-related restrictions. Paper presented at the Annual Meetings of the Southern Political Science Association (virtual meeting, January 6-9).

Woodward, B. (2020). *Rage*. Simon and Schuster.

10 Is Southern Policy Making Distinct?

The issue of southern distinctiveness has been at the forefront of the study of southern politics since the publication of V.O. Key's seminal work *Southern Politics in State and Nation* (1949). The history of the South suggests a common bond between southern states, but is this bond different enough to declare that the South is, indeed, different from the rest of the nation? Southerners think of themselves as distinct in terms of culture, history, food, and language (accent) (see Cooper & Knotts, 2017), but do these cultural differences translate into policy differences? Cooper and Knotts point out that "southern culture" is more a state of mind than anything else and note that elements of southern culture may be found in states all around the nation. But does this translate into differences in public policy choices?

As noted in the early chapters of this volume, a significant body of work exists that addresses the question of the political distinctiveness of the South. In fact, political distinctiveness is, in essence, the heart of the extant work in southern politics. While this question is certainly of interest, a focus solely on political outcomes provides, at best, an incomplete picture of southern distinctiveness. Missing from these studies is the answer to an important question: so what? What are the implications of any southern distinctiveness we might detect in southern politics? In his well-known policy primer, James Anderson (2015, p. 7) defines "public policy" as "a purposive course of action or inaction followed by an actor or set of actors in dealing with a problem or matter of concern." Put another way, policy is the output of politics. If southern politics are truly distinct, then we would expect the outputs of that process (policy) also to be distinct in detectable ways. On the other hand, if policy outputs are not distinct in the South, does it matter whether the politics of the South are distinct?

DOI: 10.4324/9781003134602-10

A Look at the Evidence

The policy areas chosen for this book represent a cross-section of common policy questions in all 50 states. While clearly not an exhaustive list of policy questions, the policy topics included in this volume – firearm legislation, implementation of the Affordable Care Act (ACA), reproductive rights for women, clean water funding, fatal police shootings, and COVID restrictions – represent a reasonably broad range of policy arenas. States treat these policy arenas differently, and policy makers are more or less interested in these arenas across the 50 states. Still, all states have addressed the policy questions represented in our six analytical chapters and have arrived at some sort of policy decision in each area.

In four of the six policy arenas examined in this volume, the "South" dummy variable in the baseline models is statistically significant; the only two models for which this is not the case are fatal police encounters and COVID restrictions. A comparison of the "South" and "non-South" models also reveals some important differences in the independent and control variables that are significant in each model, particularly in some of the variables specific to that policy arena. For example, when looking at the Affordable Care Act (ACA) models, both insurance coverage and the health index were significantly different between the South and the non-South. For reproductive rights, three of the five independent variables (percent Evangelical, percent Jewish, and percent metropolitan) were statistically different. The evidence is more mixed in the models for water quality, fatal police encounters, and COVID restrictions; the majority of the independent variables in each model did not differ much from the South to the non-South.

Of our base model variables, the consistently best predictor was the poverty measure, which differed between South and non-South in all the models in which it was included (it was not included in the water quality model). The political variables (Republican governor; Republican legislature, and citizen ideology) were nearly evenly split in terms of the differences between the South and the non-South. The explained variance in the models also varied widely, a consequence of using the same base model for each policy arena. The goal was not to maximize the explained variance, but rather to test the efficacy of a common base model, modified with policy-specific variables, to detect any differences between the South and the non-South. In this regard, our models indicate the dimensions in each policy arena in which the South differs from the rest of the nation, and the dimension on which there seems to be less variation.

Making Sense of the Evidence

What can we conclude from this evidence? In short, the South remains distinct in terms of some policy choices, and not so distinct for others. As noted above, the "South" dummy variable was significant in four of the six baseline models, which suggests that the South retains a fair degree of distinctiveness. A closer look at each of the models reveals several subtle distinctions. The South is the most distinct in terms of restrictions on reproductive rights for women; 9 of the 12 variables in the model differ between the South and non-South. The mean of the dependent variable differs significantly; the South is more restrictive, and there is little variation among the southern states on this variable. There is also a great deal of variation across this variable in non-southern states. ACA implementation is another policy arena in which the South is clearly distinct. The ACA was opposed almost universally by every southern state; at the time of implementation, the Republican party dominated state government in nearly every southern state.

The South is least distinct in clean water policy and fatal police encounters. In spite of earlier evidence suggesting the South consisted mostly of "laggard states" (see Lester & Lombard, 1990), and evidence that the South was different in terms of clean water policy (see Breaux et al., 2010), it appears that the gap between southern states and the rest of the nation in clean water policy has narrowed in the 21st century—the gap still exists, but it is perhaps not as clear as it was in the first 25 years of the Clean Water Act. Our models for fatal police violence present some of the more interesting findings of the analytical chapters. The base, non-South, and South models are similar in terms of explained variance but the significance of predictors in the base and non-South models differ substantially when compared to the South. Outside of the South, violent offender purchase regulations and "may issue" laws are strongly significant in predicting policy restrictiveness. Interestingly, within the South, there is so little variation between the contextual variables that they were omitted from the final analysis. Each state effectively took the same stance on each of the issues across the reviewed timeframe. The findings illustrate less about policy drivers and more about the region and uniformity of the political culture in response to firearm restrictiveness.

Overall, our evidence suggests that the South remains distinct as a region, although this exceptional nature is more nuanced than we originally presumed. Politics thus do matter, in that the conduct of politics does lead to different policy choices. The relative lack of variation across the South in terms of party control and ideology would lead one to expect a certain homogeneity in policy choices, and in this regard, the South does not disappoint. However, the dominant political party in the South over the last two decades, the Republican party, is closely aligned in many ways with the national Republican party. This particular brand of Republicanism has also tended to be dominant in non-South states, and the move toward a more conservative brand of Republicanism has mirrored southern ideology. The party realignment in the South (see McKee, 2019) as a result of Nixon's southern strategy (see Maxwell & Shields, 2019) has resulted, in many respects, in a nationalization of the southern brand of conservatism. In essence, the success of this strategy has had the effect of lessening the distinctions between policy choices in the South and the non-South.

Some Final Thoughts

One of V.O. Key's (1949) primary observations was that while the South seemed distinct from the rest of the nation, differences *between* southern states were vital to an understanding of southern politics. Key's description of the southern states is not so much akin to eleven identical siblings, but rather a collection of close relatives, sharing a political DNA, having often strong genetic cultural connections, but each distinct in their individual personalities and quirks. The differences in the states, and between regions within states, complicate the picture further. If this variation within the South (and even within states) is prevalent, how can the South be distinct from the rest of the nation? The question of the political differences between the South and the rest of the nation are not just theoretical; the answer has impacts well beyond the South, as the success of the Republican Party's "long southern strategy" (Maxwell & Shields, 2019) demonstrates. The ability of the Republican Party to appeal to southern voters has had a profound effect on presidential electoral outcomes since the 1940s. As in-migration to the South continues, and populations decline in the Rust Belt states, the political importance of the South will continue to grow.

The combination of the "long southern strategy" and demographic changes in the South also raise another conundrum: is the South becoming more like the rest of the nation, or is the rest of the nation becoming more like the South? As Cooper and Knotts (2017) observe, southern identity is resilient, but is also found in places outside the South, albeit, perhaps, as a transplant rather than naturally occurring from a historical foundation. Moreover, it appears that migrants to the South have little difficulty adopting southern cultural, and perhaps political, norms. This would suggest that regionalism does matter and remains a strong force. At the same time, the South, at least in political terms, is not as monolithic as it once was. States such as Virginia, North Carolina, and, in 2020, Georgia, have experienced electoral outcomes that seem to fly in the face of expectations. The 2020 presidential election, along with the runoff races for Georgia's two Senate seats (held in January 2021), were close elections in which Democrats ultimately prevailed. In all cases, the races were decided on the strength of the urban vote, particularly in metropolitan Atlanta, Savannah, and Macon. Not coincidentally, these are areas of the state that have experienced the highest rates of in-migration, and also some of the highest concentrations of African American voters.

Key (1949) noted this trend in the Rim South in the conclusion of his book. Progressivism in North Carolina and Virginia, coupled with the growth of industry and trade in Texas[1]and development in Florida, meant that politics in the South was changing. Key was not so optimistic about the Deep South states (South Carolina, Georgia, Alabama, Mississippi, and Louisiana); he saw the issue of race as much more prevalent in those states. While our analyses do not attempt to parse differences between policy choices in the Rim South and the Deep South, anecdotal evidence suggests that the differences between these subregions noted by Key also become a factor in the mixed findings we report here. This is particularly evident examining the policy decisions in Virginia, North Carolina, and Louisiana, each with Democratic governors. With Democratic leadership in the executive and legislative branches, Virginia has taken a much more progressive turn in recent years including proactively expanding Medicaid prior to much of the rest of the region and taking additional expansive policy positions. In North Carolina and Louisiana, with split executive and legislative leadership, the progressive policies espoused by the chief executives have been largely curtailed by Republican legislatures, which in our analysis have been more frequently found to be significant in predicting policy opposition than state governorship or other political variables.

There is some evidence that – at least in terms of policy – the rest of the nation may be becoming more like the South. Breaux et al. (1998) noted this effect in terms of state policy choices in the Temporary Assistance for Needy Families (TANF) program. They note that the national TANF program bore a strong resemblance to the waiver program run by Mississippi under the precursor to TANF, Aid for Families with Dependent Children (AFDC). Mississippi ran the most restrictive program in the country, and the restrictions in the Mississippi waiver package were nearly identical to the program requirement in the TANF program. The attitudes toward government programs, welfare, and race in Mississippi were clearly attractive to national policy makers in the mid-1990s, and these attitudes are reflected in the 1996 TANF legislation. More recently, state adoption of new voter restrictions seems to be following a similar pattern. The movement toward voter ID laws began with Florida, and southern states were early adopters of voter ID laws. Following the 2020 election, some 43 states saw the introduction of new laws to further restrict voting (Brennan Center, 2021); while these attempts went well beyond the South, as of this writing the laws were advancing most quickly in southern states.

As we move firmly into the 21st century, we find ourselves in a different world than that captured by V.O. Key in the 1940s. The South has indeed changed, yet that change is tempered by the underlying conservatism of the South and the attractiveness of southern culture (Cooper & Knotts, 2017). Although Key (1984, p. 664) described the pace of change in the South as "glacial," changes in both politics and policy choices are evident in the South. Whether one adopts the conclusion of the "Americanization of the South" or its rival position, the "southernization of America," the South is less distinctive from the rest of the nation than it once was. In spite of this growing heterogeneity, the South still matters, both culturally and politically.

Note

1 Texas also experienced a positive unidirectional rise in Latino voters – almost all of them of Mexican heritage – who tend to lean fairly heavily to the Democrats. This is in contrast to Florida, where the picture is far more muddled by people of Puerto Rican, Nicaraguan, and Salvadoran heritage, and three or more generations of voters of Cuban heritage, all of differing, and not always consistent, partisan preferences.

References

Anderson, J. (2015). *Public policymaking* (8th ed.). Cengage Learning.

Breaux, D., Duncan, C., Keller, C., & Morris, J. (1998). Blazing the TANF trail: The southern mind and welfare reform in Mississippi. *American Review of Politics, 19*(Summer), 175–189.

Breaux, D., Emison, G., Morris, J., & Travis, R. (2010). State commitment to environmental quality in the South: A regional analysis. In G. Emison & J. Morris (Eds.), *Speaking green with a southern accent: Environmental management and innovation in the South* (pp. 19–33). Lexington Books.

Brennan Center for Justice. (2021). State voting laws. https://www.brennancenter .org/issues/ensure-every-american-can-vote/voting-reform/state-voting-laws

Cooper, C., & Knotts, H. (2017). *The resilience of southern identity: Why the South still matters in the minds of its people.* University of North Carolina Press.

Key, V.O. (1949). *Southern politics in state and nation.* University of Alabama Press.

Key, V.O. (1984). *Southern politics in state and nation: A new edition.* University of Tennessee Press.

Lester, J., & Lombard, E. (1990). The comparative analysis of state environmental policy. *Natural Resources Journal, 30*, 301–319.

Maxwell, A., & Shields, T. (2019). *The long southern strategy: How chasing white voters in the South changed American politics.* Oxford University Press.

McKee, S. (2019). *The dynamics of southern politics: Causes and consequences.* Sage.

Index

Note: Page numbers in **bold** denote tables.

For Product Safety Concerns and Information please contact our EU
representative GPSR@taylorandfrancis.com
Taylor & Francis Verlag GmbH, Kaufingerstraße 24, 80331 München, Germany

www.ingramcontent.com/pod-product-compliance
Lightning Source LLC
Chambersburg PA
CBHW061753270326
41928CB00011B/2491